BOSNIA

What Went Wrong?

Foreign Affairs Readers

A New Europe? (1998)
The Rise of China (1998)
Is Global Capitalism Working? (1998)
Asia: Rising or Falling? (1998)
Democracy (1998)
Bosnia: What Went Wrong? (1998)

Foreign Affairs Agenda: The New Shape of World Politics (1997)
The Marshall Plan and Its Legacy (1997)
Clash of Civilizations: The Debate (1996)
Competitiveness: An International Economics Reader (1994)

For information, or to order Foreign Affairs Readers, visit www.foreignaffairs.org.

BOSNIA
What Went Wrong?

Warren Zimmermann
William Pfaff
David Gompert
Richard Holbrooke
Charles G. Boyd
Misha Glenny
Warren Bass
Aleksa Djilas

A FOREIGN AFFAIRS READER

Printed in the United States of America.

For information on Foreign Affairs *Readers, visit www.foreignaffairs.org or email ForAff@cfr.org.*

A FOREIGN AFFAIRS READER

ISBN: 0-87609-241-5

CONTENTS

Introduction

Foreign Affairs *Readers bring together important essays first published in* Foreign Affairs. *We include a variety of articles, serving different purposes. Some may be pieces of reportage, others may strongly argue a specific point of view, still others may be statesmen's memoirs.*

Each volume presents a structured, focused set of our best essays on a specific topic. Both the topic and the essays have been chosen with a particular purpose in mind – classroom use. Most of the essays advance a thesis or provide important information that is likely to stimulate students to think and discuss the broader subject. Some are current, others were written a while ago. The latter are included because the arguments they advance are still crucial to understanding the issues. We exclude many articles, which, while excellent in other respects, might not contribute as much to discussion in the classroom.

For over 75 years, Foreign Affairs *has prided itself on publishing only the very best analytic writing on political, economic, and social trends around the globe. We hope that this collection succeeds in linking scholarship and the reality of today's world.*

A complete listing of Foreign Affairs *Readers appears at the front of this volume.*

The Last Ambassador

A Memoir of the Collapse of Yugoslavia

Warren Zimmermann

In early 1989, shortly after I was confirmed as the new—and as it turned out the last—U.S. ambassador to Yugoslavia, I sought out Lawrence Eagleburger. Eagleburger had been named deputy secretary of state for the incoming Bush administration but had not yet been approved by the Senate. His temporary office was in the small back room adjoining the opulent deputy secretary's office, and there he could be found inhaling a cigarette, which, as an asthma sufferer, he was not supposed to have.

Larry Eagleburger remains one of the foremost American experts on the Balkans. Like an unusually large number of Foreign Service officers—myself included—he served twice in Yugoslavia. He and I shared a love of the country and its people. As we talked, we discovered a mutual view that the traditional American approach to Yugoslavia no longer made sense, given the revolutionary changes sweeping Europe.

By 1989 the world had changed dramatically. The Cold War was over and the Soviet Union was breaking up. The East European countries had already slipped Moscow's leash, and Poland and Hungary had achieved quasi-Western political systems, with Czechoslovakia soon to follow. In such circumstances, Eagleburger and I agreed that in my introductory calls in Belgrade and the republican capitals, I would deliver a new message: Yugoslavia no longer enjoyed the geopolitical importance that the United States had given it during the Cold War. Then, Marshal Josip Tito had made Yugoslavia a model for independence from the Soviet Union as well as for a brand of communism that was more open politically and less centralized economically.

Now Yugoslavia had been surpassed by both Poland and Hungary in economic and political openness. In addition, human rights had become a major element of U.S. policy, and Yugoslavia's record on that issue was not good—particularly in the province of Kosovo, where an authoritarian Serbian regime was systematically depriving the Albanian majority of its basic civil liberties.

WARREN ZIMMERMANN was Ambassador to Yugoslavia from 1989 to 1992. He is now a Senior Consultant at RAND.

Finally, I was to reassert the traditional mantra of U.S. support for Yugoslavia's unity, independence, and territorial integrity. But I would add that the United States could only support unity in the context of democracy; it would strongly oppose unity imposed or preserved by force.

Thus equipped, my wife and I arrived in Belgrade on March 9, 1989, after an absence of 21 years. The city had not changed much from the dusty half-Slav, half-Turkish town we remembered. Everybody still talked politics in the outdoor cafés, shaded by splendid chestnut trees. Belgrade was an acquired taste, and I had acquired it. What had changed was the character of the Serbian politics that people were busy discussing. Slobodan Milošević, an ambitious and ruthless communist party official, had clawed his way to power several years before. In early 1989, his efforts were focused on Kosovo.

Kosovo is to Serbs what Jerusalem is to Jews—a sacred ancestral homeland. In the postwar period, the Albanians in Kosovo—about 90 percent of the population—had carved out a dominant position in the province. Milošević was intent on wresting back that control, and he had no qualms about doing it unconstitutionally. Working through the intimidating powers of the communist apparatus, he took over or suspended Kosovo's governing bodies. He replaced bureaucratic and party incumbents with Serbs or pliant Albanians, one of whom, party chief Rahman Morina, sweated through his shirt during each of my meetings with him. Morina was later carried off prematurely by a heart attack brought on, no doubt, by stress.

On Kosovo, the message that Eagleburger and I had worked out was simple: if Yugoslavia wanted to continue its close relations with the United States, it would have to curb human rights abuses in the province. The point was naturally welcomed by the Albanians in Kosovo and also by Slovenia, an already democratic republic, which was proclaiming that Kosovo was the most egregious example of Milošević's dictatorial rule. Milošević, on the other hand, took my criticism personally; he later cited it as the reason he waited nearly a year before agreeing to meet me.

AN OBSESSION WITH HISTORY

Milošević's Serbia was at the heart of the complex of issues that destroyed Yugoslavia. Serbs are a naturally talented and ebullient people with an instinctive liking for Americans that is based partly on a shared garrulity and partly on a military alliance spanning both world wars. Their tragic defect is an obsession with their own history; their hearts are in the past, not the future. In the Balkans, intellectuals tend to be the standard-bearers of nationalism; in Serbia, this is carried to fetishistic lengths.

A lugubrious, paranoid, and Serbocentric view of the past enables the Serbs to blame everyone but themselves for whatever goes wrong. They had a real grievance against Tito, in some measure justified, for creating a postwar Yugoslavia that denied them a role that they believed their large population (40 percent of the nation—similar to Russians in the old Soviet Union) and historical mission entitled them. When Tito died, leaving a Yugoslavia too decentralized for any eth-

Slobodan Milošević

Alija Izetbegović

JOVANOVIC, YUGOSLAVIA: CARTOONISTS & WRITER'S GUILD

nic group to dominate, it became inevitable that a Serbian nationalist would rise up to redress the perceived wrongs dealt his people. It was a tragedy for Serbia, its neighbors, and Europe as a whole that the nationalist turned out to be Slobodan Milošević.

After the year from the spring of 1989 to 1990 in which Milošević left me cooling my heels, I grew to know him well. We had many long conversations, all of them contentious but none of them shouting matches. "You see, Mr. Zimmermann," he would say, "only we Serbs really believe in Yugoslavia. We're not trying to secede like the Croats and Slovenes and we're not trying to create an Islamic state like the Muslims in Bosnia. They all fought against you in World War II. We were your allies." On Kosovo, Milošević painted a picture without shadings: "Kosovo has always been Serbian, except for a brief period during World War II. Yet we have given the Albanians their own government, their own parliament, their own national library, and their own schools [none of these assertions was true at the time he made them to me]. We have even given them their own academy of sciences. Have you Americans given your blacks their own academy of sciences?"

Milošević makes a stunning first impression on those who do not have the information to refute his often erroneous assertions. Many is the U.S. senator or congressman who has reeled out of his office exclaiming, "Why, he's not nearly as bad as I expected!" One congressman even invited him to a White House prayer breakfast. Milošević knows how to act with Americans. He dresses in the Western style (he spent considerable time in New York in his banking days), drinks Scotch on the rocks, and smokes Italian cigarillos. His cherubic cheeks do not fit the strongman image; in fact, he has to work hard at looking tough for his public posters. His manner is affable and displays his light side. Unfortunately, the man is almost totally dominated by his dark side.

Radovan Karadžić

Franjo Tudjman

Milošević began his career as a communist apparatchik of extremely authoritarian mien, even for Serbia. He rose to the leadership of the Serbian party by betraying the man who gave him his chance in politics, Ivan Stambolić, whose purge Milošević organized. Milošević is an opportunist, not an ideologue, a man driven by power rather than nationalism. He has made a Faustian pact with nationalism as a way to gain and hold power.

He is a man of extraordinary coldness. I never saw him moved by an individual case of human suffering; for him, people are groups (Serbs, Muslims) or simply abstractions. Nor did I ever hear him say a charitable or generous word about any human being, not even a Serb. This chilling personality trait made it possible for Milošević to condone, encourage, and even organize the unspeakable atrocities committed by Serbian citizens in the Bosnian war. It also accounts for his habitual mendacity, as in his outrageous distortion of Serbian behavior in Kosovo. For Milošević, truth has only a relative value. If it serves his objectives, it is employed; if not, it can be discarded.

When the unity of Yugoslavia was threatened in the late 1980s by Slovenia—Yugoslavia's only Serbless republic—Milošević cast himself as the apostle of unity. Not interested in unity per se, he wanted a unity that Serbia could dominate, working through the Yugoslav People's Army, whose officer corps was over 50 percent Serbian. Milošević's concept of unity did not extend to democracy or power-sharing with other national groups.

In fact, in his verbal attacks on Slovenia and Croatia and his subsequent trade sanctions against them, he became the major wrecker of Yugoslavia. When the Slovenian and Croatian independence movements, together with Milošević's own disruptive actions in the name of unity, made the preservation of Yugoslavia impossible, he fell back on an even more aggressive approach. If Yugoslavia could not encompass all Serbs, then Serbia would. The Serbian populations of Croatia, Bosnia, Montenegro, and possibly Macedonia would be incorporated—along with generous pieces of territory—into a Milošević-dominated "Yugoslavia." His rallying cry was that all Serbs have the right to live in a single state—a doctrine that, if applied globally, would cause the disintegration of dozens of multinational states.

WORST-CASE SCENARIOS

From the beginning of my ambassadorship in Yugoslavia, I pressed the talented and highly professional group of political and economic officers in the U.S. embassy in Belgrade and the consulate general in Zagreb, Croatia, to consider worst-case scenarios for Yugoslavia. The worst case we could think of was the breakup of the country. We reported to Washington that no breakup of Yugoslavia could happen peacefully. The ethnic hatred sown by Milošević and his ilk and the mixture of ethnic groups in every republic except Slovenia meant that Yugoslavia's shattering would lead to extreme violence, perhaps even war. Thus we favored at least a loose unity while encouraging democratic development. The new Yugoslav prime minister, Ante Marković, a dynamic Croatian committed to economic reform and other Western policies, was pressing for both these objectives. The United States supported him and persuaded the West European governments to do so as well.

The U.S. policy of unity and democracy was not controversial within the Bush administration or initially in Western Europe. But it faced vehement criticism, led by Senator Robert Dole (R-Kans.), in the U.S. Congress. Critics of the policy charged that our efforts to hold together a country that was falling apart helped Milošević and hurt the democratic forces in Slovenia and Croatia. The critics did not understand that democratic unity favored Marković, not Milošević, who had no interest in unity on a democratic reformist basis. In the end, the dissolution of Yugoslavia did lead to war (and to Serbian territorial gains), and thus confirmed that unity and democracy were the Siamese twins of Yugoslavia's fate. The loss of one meant that the other would die.

In January 1990, the communist party created by Tito breathed its last; a party congress split by quarreling was adjourned, never to meet again. Yugoslavia lurched into its first democratic elections. The two most anti-Yugoslav republics, Slovenia and Croatia, were the first to vote. By the end of the year the four southern republics had voted as well. Even the Serbian government held elections, despite Milošević's occasional assertions to me that Serbia's needs were much better met by a one-party system.

The republican elections turned out to be a disaster for those who hoped to keep Yugoslavia together in a democratic framework. People had no opportunity to vote on a Yugoslavia-wide level once Prime Minister Marković failed to win approval for federal elections. They vented their pent-up frustrations by voting for nationalists who hammered on ethnic themes. The elections became a test of ethnic loyalty. Ethnic parties won power in five of the six republics, all but Macedonia.

NATIONALISM UNLEASHED

By bringing nationalism to power almost everywhere, the elections helped snuff out the very flame of democracy that they had kindled. Nationalism is by nature uncivil, antidemocratic, and separatist because it empowers one ethnic group over all others. If the elections weakened the democratic element so necessary for Yugoslavia, they also weakened the necessary unifying element. I visited all six republics to evaluate the new leaders. I found that not only was the country breaking up into different power centers, but each local region was developing a nationalist ideology, each different from the other. The age of naked nationalism had begun.

Slovenian nationalists, now in power, quickly broke almost all Slovenia's remaining political and economic ties with the Yugoslav government. The Slovenes' separatist nationalism was unique in Yugoslavia—it had no victims and no enemies; while the Slovenes hated Milošević, they built no ideology against him. They practiced a "Garbo nationalism"—they just wanted to be left alone. Their virtue was democracy and their vice was selfishness. In their drive to separate from Yugoslavia they simply ignored the 22 million Yugoslavs who were not Slovenes. They bear considerable responsibility for the bloodbath that followed their secession.

No Yugoslav republic was more transformed by the elections of 1990 than Croatia. The decisive victory of the Croatian Democratic Union in May brought to the presidency an implacable nationalist, Franjo Tudjman. I first met Tudjman in Zagreb on the morning of his victory; before then I had avoided him because of the extreme nature of some of his campaign statements. If Milošević recalls a slick con man, Tudjman resembles an inflexible schoolteacher. He is a former general and communist, expelled from the party under Tito and twice jailed for nationalism. Prim steel eyeglasses hang on a square face whose natural expression is a scowl. His mouth occasionally creases into a nervous chuckle or mirthless laugh. In our first meeting, he treated the colleagues who accompanied him with extreme disdain. Then, on the spot, he appointed two of them to high-ranking positions—to their surprise, since the venue for this solemn act was the breakfast table of the American consul general.

Tudjman's temper flared when I asked him about his remark during the campaign that he was glad his wife was neither a Serb nor a Jew. He launched into a ten-minute defense of his ethnic humanity, claiming, among other things, that some of his best friends were Serbs. While he didn't profess similar affinities with Jews (and his earlier writings had denigrated the Holocaust), he did promise to make restitution to the Zagreb Jewish community for the destruction of its synagogue by Croatian fascists during World War II. He kept that promise.

Unlike Milošević, who is driven by power, Tudjman is obsessed by nationalism. His devotion to Croatia is of the most narrow-minded sort, and he has never shown much understanding of or interest in democratic values. He presided over serious violations of the rights of Serbs, who made up 12 percent of the population of Croatia. They were dismissed from work, required to take loyalty oaths, and subjected to attacks on their homes and property. I have sat at Tudjman's lunch table and listened to several of his ministers revile Serbs in the most racist terms. He didn't join in, but he didn't stop them either. He has also stifled the independence of the press as much as Milošević, and maybe even more.

Tudjman's saving grace, which distinguishes him from Milošević, is that he really wants to be a Western statesman. He therefore listens to Western expressions of concern and criticism and often does something about them. For better or worse, Croatian nationalism is defined by Tudjman—intolerant, anti-Serb, and authoritarian. These attributes—together with an aura of wartime fascism, which Tudjman has done nothing to dispel—help explain why many Serbs in Croatia reject Croatian rule and why the core hostility in the former Yugoslavia is still between Serbs and Croats.

During 1990, Serbian nationalism under Milošević became even more aggressive. No longer was it enough for Serbs living outside Serbia to have their rights protected. They also had to own and control the territory they inhabited, regardless of prior sovereignty. These Serbian claims had no consistent principles behind them. Where Serbs were a minority, as in Kosovo, they asserted a historical, rather than a numerical, right to rule. Where no such historical right was plausible, as in the Krajina area of Croatia, they claimed self-determination on the majority principle. Revealingly, Milošević was unwilling to give the Albanians in Kosovo the same right of self-determination that he demanded for Serbs in Croatia and Bosnia.

In the Serbian elections of December 1990, Milošević made nationalism the litmus test: if you didn't vote for him, you were not a good Serb. The Serbian opposition, overwhelmed by the superior organization of Milošević's still-intact communist apparatus and a near-total media blackout, foundered on whether to play the nationalist game or reject it. Milošević won in a tainted but convincing landslide. The one-party system, beloved by the Serbian leader, survived. Milošević simply modernized it by giving it multiparty trimmings.

Albanian nationalism was, like Croatian nationalism, to some degree a reaction to Milošević's aggressive tactics. As the Serbs pressed, the Albanians stiffened. They boycotted the Serbian elections, despite U.S. counsel that a determined parliamentary minority could wield much political leverage. Milošević's strong-arm approach had launched the Albanians on a path of no return toward complete independence from the Serbs.

By December 1990, there were few Kosovo Albanians who did not insist either on an independent Kosovo or a Kosovo linked with Albania. The psychological break was complete. Any provocation launched by either side had the potential to blow the province apart. In these volatile circumstances, I urged Milošević to meet with the disciplined and impressive Albanian leader Ibrahim Rugova, who was urging a policy of peaceful resistance. Rugova agreed. Milošević refused, saying of the leader of some two million Albanian subjects of Serbia, "Who does he represent?"

The most interesting opposition figure in Serbia was Vuk Drašković, a flamboyant and talented novelist, who leaped onto the political stage as a pro-Serbian extremist, complete with Old Testament beard, racist ideas, and the persona of a Serbian peasant. Once he found his political sea legs, however, Drašković turned into a staunch defender of an open political system and free press. On March 9, 1991, he used his talent for motivating people to stage a mass rally in Belgrade against Milošević's control of the press. Clumsy handling by the police and the army led to two deaths—a demonstrator and a policeman—and to Drašković's arrest and brief detention. Many observers felt that the rally, which has now entered Serbian folklore, came close to dethroning Milošević. While this is doubtful, the courage of nearly 100,000 spontaneous demonstrators was a moving tribute to the democratic vibrancy of many Serbs.

Many new opposition figures within the former republics of Yugoslavia took a clear stand against nationalism. In speaking out, they paid a price in ransacked offices, bombings, death threats, beatings, and arrests. With my strong support, Western human rights groups helped many opposition organizations and publications to survive. The investment, however long-term, will pay off one day. The people being helped, and those who will succeed them, are part of the "other Serbia" and the "other Croatia"—the core of the democratic revival that in time must replace the current nationalist hysteria.

Neither Milošević nor Tudjman could understand why we cared so much about people who were murdered, tortured, abused, or harassed. Milošević would listen patiently, then ask, "Why do you waste time on these individuals, who are mostly criminals anyway, when Serbs as a nation have been abused for years?" Tudjman would often erupt in fury when I had the temerity to suggest that Croatian authorities were not always model democrats. When it came to results, however, Milošević almost never delivered; Tudjman sometimes did.

ELEVENTH-HOUR MANEUVERS

The last year of Yugoslavia's existence—1991—saw the unfolding of unilateral and conflicting nationalist strategies. Slovenia, where a December 1990 referendum showed overwhelming popular support for independence, announced its decision to secede in June 1991 if a loose confederal solution was not found. Wittingly making his republic a hostage to Slovenian policy, Tudjman said Croatia would do what Slovenia did. Milošević countered that the breakup of Yugoslavia would lead to Serbia's incorporating all Serbs into a single state. Bosnian leader Alija Izetbegović argued that the survival of Yugoslavia in some form was essential to Bosnia's survival as well.

Izetbegović was mild-mannered, deferential, and perpetually anxious; he wore the mantle of leadership with great discomfort. A devout Muslim but no extremist, he consistently advocated the preservation of a multinational Bosnia. Ironically, it was Milošević and Tudjman, in their professed desire for Bosnian Serbs and Bosnian Croats to live apart from Muslims, who laid the philosophical groundwork for a separate Muslim entity. Bosnia had a strong multiethnic character and the highest percentage of ethnically mixed marriages of any republic. While its history since the fifteenth-century Turkish occupation was no more bloody than the history of England or France, Bosnia was the major Balkan killing ground during World War II. Izetbegović was succinct with me: "If Croatia goes independent, Bosnia will be destroyed."

In early 1991, the supporters of a unified and democratic Yugoslavia were becoming marginalized. The leaders of the two republics with the most to lose from the breakup of Yugoslavia—Alija Izetbegović of Bosnia and Kiro Gligorov of Macedonia—proposed to hold it together in an even weaker configuration. Milošević gave their plan lip service; the Croats and Slovenes rejected it flatly for leaving too many powers with the central government.

During this period the Yugoslav People's Army (JNA in its Serbo-Croatian acronym) emerged as a major political player, an unusual role for a communist army. I met regularly with the defense minister, General Veljko Kadijević, a brooding, humorless officer who spoke with antipathy about Slovenes and Croats and with paranoia about Germans, whom he saw as bent on incorporating the Balkans into a Fourth Reich. The JNA enjoyed a proud tradition, with roots in Tito's Partisan fighters, who stood up to the Germans in World War II. The fifth-largest army in Europe, well supplied by the Soviet Union and an enormous domestic arms industry, it was seen by many as the most important unifying institution in Yugoslavia. Its officer corps, however, had a Serbian majority who, when events forced them to choose, followed Milošević.

The JNA was soon on a collision course with the breakaway republics. Both Croatia and Slovenia were trying to create their own military forces by calling on their young men to desert the JNA and by weakening the JNA's control over the republican Territorial Defense Forces, a sort of national guard. The JNA went berserk over this proliferation of armies. "How many armies does the United States have?" Kadijević stormed at me. In early 1991, the JNA tried to force the Yugoslav presidency—a comically weak, collective, eight-person chief of state—to declare a national emergency and authorize the army to disarm the Slovenian and Croatian militaries. This bid, which amounted to a military coup, was frustrated politically by the democratically inclined presidency members from Macedonia and Slovenia, Vasil Tupurkovski and Janez Drnovšek. The defeat led Milošević to use the four votes he controlled in the eight-member presidency to subvert the scheduled rotation of its "president" from a Serb to a Croat. I asked Milošević several days before the May 15 election by the presidency if he would block the accession of the Croat Stipe Mesić, even though it was called for by constitutional precedent. "Serbia will always act in the spirit of the highest democratic principles," replied Milošević, who was always at his most mellifluous when expatiating on his devotion to democracy. "There will be a democratic vote in the presidency."

"But are you going to accept a fair transition from a Serb to a Croat president?" I pursued. "Mr. Zimmermann," he said, "you can tell your government that it has absolutely nothing to worry about." I cabled Washington that Mesić was not a sure thing. Two days later Milošević's allies on the presidency blocked Mesić's ascension, throwing Yugoslavia into a constitutional crisis. When I accused Milošević later of lying to me, he asserted that he had not actually promised that Mesić would be named. The incident illustrated three important traits of Milošević's character: his cynicism about Yugoslavia's unity and institutions, his natural mendacity, and the pains he always took to avoid direct responsibility for aggressive actions. The third trait was to become particularly relevant to Milošević's hidden hand in the Bosnia crisis.

ENTER BAKER

It was in the context of Milošević's move against the Yugoslav presidency and its Croatian president-designate, Croatian actions against the jobs and property of Serbs in Croatia, growing violence between Serbs and Croats, and the threat by both Slovenia and Croatia to withdraw from Yugoslavia at midyear that Secretary of State James Baker arrived in Belgrade on June 21, 1991.

During his one-day visit Baker had nine consecutive meetings: with the Albanian leaders from Kosovo, with all six republican leaders, and twice with Yugoslav Prime Minister Ante Marković and Foreign Minister Budimir Lončar. Listening to Baker deal with these complex and irascible personalities, I felt that I had rarely, if ever, heard a secretary of state make a more skillful or reasonable presentation. Baker's failure was due not to his message but to the fact that the different parts of Yugoslavia were on a collision course.

Baker expressed the American hope that Yugoslavia would hold together behind the reformist Marković, who by that time was seen increasingly as a figurehead or, even worse, a fig leaf. Baker said that it was up to the people of Yugoslavia to determine their future governing structures; the United States would support any arrangement on which they could peacefully agree. Baker told Croatian President Franjo Tudjman and Slovene President Milan Kučan that the United States would not encourage or support unilateral secession; he hoped they would not secede, but if they had to leave, he urged them to leave by negotiated agreement. He argued that self-determination cannot be unilateral but must be pursued by dialogue and peaceful means. To Milošević and (indirectly) the army, Baker made clear that the United States strongly opposed any use of force, intimidation, or incitement to violence that would block democratic change. Yugoslavia could not be held together at gunpoint. In his encounter with Milošević—the most contentious of the nine meetings—Baker hammered the Serb leader on his human rights violations in Kosovo, urged his acquiescence to a looser constitutional arrangement for Yugoslavia, and pressed him to stop destabilizing the Yugoslav presidency.

Never was a green light given or implied to Milošević or the army to invade the seceding republics, as has since been alleged in some press accounts. But was there a red light? Not as such, because the United States had given no consideration to using force to stop a Serbian/JNA attack on Slovenia or Croatia. Nor, at that point, had a single member of Congress, as far as I know, advocated the introduction of American military power. Baker did, however, leave a strong political message. He said to Prime Minister Marković, a conduit to the army, "If you force the United States to choose between unity and democracy, we will always choose democracy."

Baker's message was the right one, but it came too late. If a mistake was made, it was that the secretary of state had not come six months earlier, a time that unfortunately coincided with the massive American preparations for the Persian Gulf War. By June 1991, Baker was making a last-ditch effort. Even so, it is not clear that an earlier visit by Baker would have made a difference. The aggressive nationalism emanating like noxious fumes from the leaders of Serbia and Croatia and their even more extreme advisers, officials, media manipulators, and allies had cast the die for disintegration and violence.

The breakup of Yugoslavia is a classic example of nationalism from the top down—a manipulated nationalism in a region where peace has historically prevailed more than war and in which a quarter of the population were in mixed marriages. The manipulators condoned and even provoked local ethnic violence in order to engender animosities that could then be magnified by the press, leading to further violence. Milošević gave prime television time to fanatic nationalists like Vojislav Šešelj, who once said that the way to deal with the Kosovo Albanians was to kill them all. Tudjman also used his control of the media to sow hate. Nationalist "intellectuals," wrapped in the mantle of august academies of sciences, expounded their pseudo-history of the victimization of Serbs (or Croats) through the ages. One of them seriously asserted to me that Serbs had committed no crimes or moral transgressions at any point in their long history. Worst of all, the media, under the thumb of most republican regimes, spewed an endless daily torrent of violence and enmity. As a reporter for *Vreme*, one of the few independent magazines left in the former Yugoslavia, said, "You Americans would become nationalists and racists too if your media were totally in the hands of the Ku Klux Klan."

SECESSION AND WAR

In late June 1991, just a few days after Baker's departure from Belgrade and almost exactly according to their timetable, Croatia and Slovenia declared independence. Fighting began in Slovenia almost immediately. Contrary to the general view, it was the Slovenes who started the war. Their independence declaration, which had not been preceded by even the most token effort to negotiate, effectively put under their control all the border and customs posts between Slovenia and its two neighbors, Italy and Austria. This meant that Slovenia, the only international gateway between the West and Yugoslavia, had unilaterally appropriated the right to goods destined for other republics, as well as customs revenues estimated at some 75 percent of the Yugoslav federal budget. Even an army less primitive than the JNA would have reacted. Worst of all, the Slovenes' understandable desire to be independent condemned the rest of Yugoslavia to war.

The Yugoslav generals, thinking they could intimidate the Slovenes, roared their tanks through peaceful Slovenian streets, slapping aside compact cars as they lumbered through. The Slovenes, trained by the JNA itself in territorial defense, fought back. After ten days, at Milošević's direction or with his acquiescence, the JNA withdrew from Slovenia, leaving the republic effectively independent. Compared to the Croatian and Bosnian wars that followed, the casualty figures in Slovenia seem ludicrously small: 37 JNA and 12 Slovenes killed. They do not bear out the generally held assumption that the Yugoslav army waged an extermination campaign in Slovenia. In provoking war, the Slovenes won the support of the world's television viewers and consolidated their entire population behind independence. Unlike the JNA, they welcomed foreign journalists, to whom they retailed the epic struggle of their tiny republic against the Yugoslav colossus. It was the most brilliant public relations coup in the history of Yugoslavia.

It was no surprise to me that Milošević was willing to let Slovenia go. His policy since 1989 provoked the Slovenes to secede by making it clear that he would not tolerate their liberal, independent ways. With Slovenia out of the game, he and the JNA were now free to take on a Croatia no longer able to count on Slovenia's support.

The fighting in Croatia began with the illusion of evenhandedness. The Yugoslav army would step in to separate the Serbian and Croatian combatants. During the summer of 1991, however, it soon became clear that the JNA, while claiming neutrality, was in fact turning territory over to Serbs. The war in Croatia had become a war of aggression.

As the war grew more bitter through the summer of 1991, the European Community (EC) and the United Nations launched a joint effort to achieve a cease-fire and an agreement among all the Yugoslav republics. Special U.N. envoys Cyrus Vance and Lord Peter Carrington, two former foreign ministers and old friends, shared the Sisyphean task of achieving a peaceful outcome. The determined Vance won the trust of the JNA and succeeded on January 3, 1992, in producing a cease-fire that froze both the military and political status quo in Croatia. The fighting stopped, but the Serbs were left holding about a quarter of the republic. The freeze was unwittingly stabilized by U.N. peacekeepers who arrived in March 1992.

Carrington's job was to get the feuding Yugoslav republics to define the relationship they were prepared to have with each other. He and Vance both argued—as did the U.S. government—that there should be no Western recognition of the independence of any Yugoslav republic until all had agreed on their mutual relationships. If this simple principle had been maintained, less blood would have been shed in Bosnia.

During the fall of 1991, while Vance and Carrington were launching their diplomatic efforts, the JNA shelled the Croatian cities of Vukovar and Dubrovnik, the first major war crimes in Yugoslavia since World War II. The pretty Croatian city of Vukovar, with a mixed population, of which over a third was Serb, first came under JNA shelling in August, apparently because of its location on the Danube River between Serbia and Croatia. For three months the army, shrinking from an attack that might have cost it casualties, sat outside the city and shelled it to pieces. The civilian population of the city—Serbs and Croats alike—huddled in cellars. Over 2,000 civilians were killed before the JNA finally "liberated" the city.

One of the employees in our embassy residence, a young Croatian woman named Danijela Hajnal, was from Vukovar; her mother was trapped in a cellar during the siege. During her stay with my wife and me after Vukovar fell, Danijela's mother described the relations between Serbs and Croats during the attack: "There were a hundred people in that cellar," she said, "half of us Croats and half Serbs. We were friends when we went into the cellar, and three months later when we came out, we were still friends." About the same time I asked Danijela how many Serbs and Croats were in her high school class in Vukovar. She replied that she didn't have the faintest idea. These vignettes, which could be multiplied thousands of times over, show how natural it was for Yugoslavs to get along with each other, despite the ranting of their leaders.

Notwithstanding solemn guarantees by General Kadijević, the JNA in October 1991 also shelled Dubrovnik from the hills and the sea. This medieval town, which glowed in the Adriatic like a piece of pink marble, had withstood the depredations of Turks, Venetians, and many other would-be conquerors. Now it was falling under the guns of an army whose constitutional duty was to defend it. Dubrovnik was not destroyed, but the damage inflicted by the Yugoslav army exceeded the best efforts of any previous marauder. Only Milošević pretended that there was any military objective in Dubrovnik. Denying, as usual, any personal responsibility for what the army did, he told me with a straight face that there were foreign mercenaries hiding in the city. Kadijević didn't even pretend that Dubrovnik was a military target. "I give you my word," he told me, "that the shelling of Dubrovnik was unauthorized. Those who did it will be punished." My repeated requests for the details of their punishment went unanswered.

Shelling civilian populations is a war crime. Vukovar and Dubrovnik led directly to the merciless attacks on Sarajevo and other Bosnian cities. Yet no Western government at the time called on NATO's military force to get the JNA to stop shelling Dubrovnik, although NATO's supreme commander, General John Galvin, had prepared contingency plans for doing so. The use of force was simply too big a step to consider in late 1991. I did not recommend it myself—a major mistake. The JNA's artillery on the hills surrounding Dubrovnik and its small craft on the water would have been easy targets. Not only would damage to the city have been averted, but the Serbs would have been taught a lesson about Western resolve that might have deterred at least some of their aggression against Bosnia. As it was, the Serbs learned another lesson—that there was no Western resolve, and that they could push about as far as their power could take them.

A TAR BABY IN WASHINGTON

Secretary of State Baker's failure to head off the Slovenian and Croatian declarations of independence cooled whatever ardor he may have had for projecting the United States into the Yugoslav imbroglio. During the summer of 1991, it had been fair enough to give the EC a chance to deal with what it called a "European problem." But by autumn, the Serbian/JNA plan for taking over parts of Croatia had crystallized in the attacks on Vukovar and Dubrovnik. Threats to the integrity of Bosnia were growing, and the EC, under German cajoling, was stumbling toward recognition of the breakaway republics. Even without threatening force, the United States could have thrown more weight behind the effort to prevent greater violence. However, between July 1991 and March 1992, the United States was not a major factor in the Yugoslav crisis. In the fall of 1991, at a U.S. ambassadors' meeting in Berlin, a friend from the State Department's European Bureau told me that Yugoslavia had become a tar baby in Washington. Nobody wanted to touch it. With the American presidential election just a year away, it was seen as a loser.

Unfortunately, American immobility coincided with growing pressure on Bosnia. Neither Milošević nor Tudjman made any effort to conceal their designs on Bosnia from me. As a place where Serbs, Croats, and Muslims had coexisted more or less peacefully for centuries, Bosnia was an affront and a challenge to these two ethnic supremacists.

At the end of a long meeting with me, Tudjman erupted into a diatribe against Izetbegović and the Muslims of Bosnia. "They're dangerous fundamentalists," he charged, "and they're using Bosnia as a beachhead to spread their ideology throughout Europe and even to the United States. The civilized nations should join together to repel this threat. Bosnia has never had any real existence. It should be divided between Serbia and Croatia."

I was flabbergasted at this outburst and got the impression that Tudjman's aides who were present were equally surprised. With some heat I asked, "Mr. President, how can you expect the West to help you get back the parts of Croatia taken by the Serbs when you yourself are advancing naked and unsupported claims on a neighboring republic?" There was no answer. I added, "And how can you expect Milošević to respect a deal with you to divide Bosnia when he's trying to annex part of Croatia?" Amazingly, Tudjman answered, "Because I can trust Milošević." On the way down the stairs after this surreal discussion, I asked one of Tudjman's aides if I had gotten too emotional in defending the integrity of Bosnia. "Oh no," he said, "You were just fine."

Milošević's strategy for Bosnia, unlike Tudjman's, was calculating rather than emotional. When Slovenia and Croatia declared independence and stopped participating in the Yugoslav government, Milošević, notwithstanding all he had done to destroy Yugoslavia, now claimed to be its heir. He contended that all those who wanted to "remain" in Yugoslavia should have the right to do so. This included, of course, the Serbs of Croatia and the Serbs of Bosnia. As Milošević explained this to me, he added that while the Muslims in Bosnia tended to live in cities, the Serbs were a rural people living on 70 percent of the land, to which they therefore had a right. Thus, at least six months before the Bosnian Serb army and the irregulars from Serbia shattered the peace in Bosnia, Milošević was laying the groundwork for a Serbian claim. From that moment, in every conversation I had with him I emphasized the strong U.S. opposition to any Serbian power play in Bosnia.

FATAL RECOGNITION

When Croatia opted for independence in mid-1991, Bosnian President Izetbegović saw the writing on the wall for his republic. He scurried throughout Europe and the United States looking for ways to head off disaster. He pushed, without success, the dying Izetbegović-Gligorov plan for a loosely connected Yugoslavia. He asked for and got EC observers in Bosnia. He asked for, but did not get, U.N. peacekeepers there. Vance and the U.N. leadership in New York took the traditional if puzzling line that peacekeepers are used after a conflict, not before. The U.S. government did not support Izetbegović on the request for peacekeepers either. In a cable to Washington I urged this innovative step, but did not press for it as hard as I should have. As an unsatisfactory compromise, when the U.N. peacekeepers arrived in Croatia in March 1992, they set up their headquarters in Sarajevo.

In the fall of 1991, German Foreign Minister Hans-Dietrich Genscher pressed his EC colleagues to recognize Slovenia and Croatia and to offer recognition to Bosnia and Macedonia. Izetbegović, briefed by the German ambassador to Yugoslavia on how to make his point with Genscher that EC recognition would bring violence to Bosnia, unaccountably failed to do so in his November meeting with the German foreign minister. The omission can only have led Genscher to assume that he had a green light from Izetbegović for recognition.

I was urging Washington to defer recognition, as the EC ambassadors in Belgrade were urging their governments. Although Washington was opposed to premature recognition, U.S. appeals to EC governments were perfunctory. On December 17, 1991, an EC summit decided to grant recognition. Carrington and Vance both complained loudly and publicly. The State Department's statement, to avoid ruffling the EC, was nuanced. War in Bosnia, which had until then been probable, now became virtually inevitable.

A few days after the EC's decision, I had lunch in Belgrade with Izetbegović's deputy, Ejup Ganić, a Muslim hard-liner who had trained at MIT. I asked him, "Is Bosnia really going to ask for recognition in the face of all the dangers Izetbegović has repeatedly warned about? Wouldn't it be better to tell the European Community that you need more time to work out the political issues involved?" Ganić looked at me as if I had just dropped out of the sky. He said, "Of course we're going to move ahead on recognition. With Croatia and Slovenia now gone, we can't consign Bosnia to a truncated Yugoslavia controlled by Serbia."

I concluded from the abrupt change of tack by Ganić that Izetbegović was now playing a double game. With the European Community heading toward recognition, he thought he could get away with it under the guns of the Serbs. Perhaps he counted on Western military support, though nobody had promised him that. Whatever his motives, it was a disastrous political mistake. Serbia, Bosnia's vastly more powerful neighbor, now had the pretext it needed to strike—the claim that 1.3 million Serbs were being taken out of "Yugoslavia" against their will. I believe that Milošević and Bosnian Serb leader Radovan Karadžić had already decided to annex the majority of Bosnia by military force (Milošević had spoken to me of 70 percent). The EC's irresponsibility, the United States' passivity, and Izetbegović's miscalculation made their job easier.

Events took their inexorable course following the EC's recognition decision. Hardly anybody noticed the December 20 resignation of Marković, so powerless had Yugoslavia's last prime minister become. Although defeated by an ad hoc cabal of nationalists, from the liberal Slovenes to the neo-communist Serbs, Marković still departed as a symbol of everything his country needed: a modern, stable economy, the rule of law, and ethnic tolerance. He had treated Yugoslavia like a patient with a serious cancer—nationalism. A semi-heroic, semi-tragic figure, Marković failed, but at least he had fought the cancer instead of adjusting to it. He had aspired to be Yugoslavia's savior. Instead, he turned out to be the Yugoslavian equivalent of Russia's last leader before the Bolshevik deluge, Aleksandr Kerensky. The war in Croatia, the impending war in Bosnia, and a future that promised a generation of violence in the Balkans were the results of Yugoslavia's demise.

PARTNERS IN CRIME

During the first few months of 1992, events in Bosnia careened down two parallel tracks. On one, the Izetbegović government, following the EC lead, prepared for independence. Its referendum on February 29 and March 1 produced predictable results. Practically all the Muslims and Croats voted for independence, yielding a 64-percent majority, while practically all the Serbs boycotted the election. On the other track, the leaders of the Serbian minority prepared for secession and war. Since the 1990 Bosnian election, I had paid periodic visits to Karadžić. The Bosnian Serb leader is a large man with flamboyant hair, an outwardly friendly manner, and the unlikely profession of psychiatry. In the great tradition of nationalists who do not come from their nation (Hitler, Napoleon, Stalin), Karadžić is from Montenegro, not Bosnia. I learned from experience that his outstanding characteristics were his stubbornness and deep-seated hostility to Muslims, Croats, and any other non-Serb ethnic group in his neighborhood.

I was startled to hear the extravagance of Karadžić's claims on behalf of the Serbs. He told me that "Serbs have a right to territory not only where they're now living but also where they're buried, since the earth they lie in was taken unjustly from them." When I asked whether he would accept parallel claims on behalf of Croats or Muslims, he answered, "No, because Croats are fascists and Muslims are Islamic fanatics." His disdain for the truth was absolute; he insisted that "Sarajevo is a Serbian city," which it has never been. His apartheid philosophy was as extreme as anything concocted in South Africa. He was the architect of massacres in the Muslim villages, ethnic cleansing, and artillery attacks on civilian populations. In his fanaticism, ruthlessness, and contempt for human values, he invites comparison with a monster from another generation, Heinrich Himmler.

Karadžić and Milošević both made an elaborate pretense to me of not knowing each other very well and having no operational contacts. Milošević always reacted with cherubic innocence when I accosted him over Bosnia. "But why do you come to me, Mr. Zimmermann? Serbia has nothing to do with Bosnia. It's not our problem." This fiction suited each leader—Milošević to escape responsibility for aggression, Karadžić to avoid the charge that he was a henchman of Milošević's rather than a Serbian folk hero in his own right.

There is no doubt, however, that the two were partners in war crimes. Copying Milošević's strategy in Croatia, Karadžić's followers—beginning a year before the Bosnian war broke out—declared three "Serb Autonomous Regions" in Bosnia, began an arms supply relationship with the JNA, and accepted JNA intervention in September to define their borders. They established artillery positions around Sarajevo and other towns, created a "Bosnian Serb" army (effectively a branch of the JNA, commanded by a JNA general and using JNA-supplied heavy artillery, tanks, and air power), established their own parliament, and attempted a putsch in Sarajevo on March 2, 1992. In March 1992—before any country had recognized the independence of Bosnia—they declared a "Serbian Republic." These steps, particularly those involving the JNA, would not have been possible without Milošević's direct involvement.

In response to the evidence of Serbian collusion and the results of the Bosnian referendum, and in hopes that recognition might deter a Serbian attack, the United States and other NATO countries recognized Bosnia in early April 1992. However, a few days before, Serbs had launched an attack from Serbia across the Drina River, which forms the border between Serbia and Bosnia. Milošević, Karadžić, and their spokesmen have asserted that the Western recognition of Bosnia had forced the Serbs to move. I doubt this. The two Serbian leaders already had a joint strategy for dividing Bosnia and they were going to carry it out, regardless of what the rest of the world did.

The attack on Bosnia showed that Milošević and Karadžić are apostles of the most aggressive form of nationalism. Milošević-style nationalism has proven singularly resistant to economic inducements, penalties, or any other pressures short of force. Unfortunately, neither the Bush nor the Clinton administration was willing to step up to the challenge of using force in Bosnia, despite significant American interests in the Balkans. Moreover, the two Serbian strongmen, behind their propaganda, espouse the doctrine of the single nation-state, a deeply uncivilized concept. Nation-states have nothing to unify them but their nationalism, and power within them will naturally gravitate to the most strident nationalists. Multinational states, a majority in the world, can be deeply conflicted, as Yugoslavia proves. But they can also be schools of tolerance, since the need to take account of minority interests moderates behavior. Yugoslavia had its democrats as well as its demagogues. The attackers across the Drina, however, were barbarians, pure and simple.

The Serbian attack was directed at towns with large Muslim majorities. Gangsters from Serbia proper, including the notorious Arkan, who had left a trail of murder and pillage during the Croatian war, were displayed on Belgrade television swaggering on the debris of Bijeljina and other Muslim towns. Those Serbia-based marauders accounted for the high volume of atrocities committed in the early days of the war—the gang rapes, ethnic cleansing, and wanton murder of Muslim villagers. The presence in Bosnia of irregulars from Serbia drained all credibility from Milošević's assertion that Serbia had nothing to do with what was going on there.

During one of the meetings in which, on Washington's instructions, I accused Milošević of aggression in Bosnia, he asserted, "There isn't a single Serb from Serbia involved in the fighting in Bosnia."

"But," I said, "I saw Arkan on your own Belgrade television boasting about his capture of Bosnian villages."

"Our television is free to broadcast whatever it wants," said Milošević. "You shouldn't take it so seriously. Besides, you needn't worry about trouble in Bosnia. Serbs have no serious grievances in Bosnia; they're not being abused there. This is a big difference with Serbs in Croatia." Via this backhanded compliment to the Izetbegović government, Milošević reduced the Serbian argument for naked aggression to the assumption that Serbs had a right to murder, torture, and expel simply because they did not want to live under an independent multiethnic government that was not abusing them.

LAST WORDS

Just a few weeks before I was recalled in protest against the Serbian aggression in Bosnia, I had my last talk with Karadžić in Belgrade, where he was pretending not to see Milošević. He came to the U.S. embassy, bringing with him as usual his deputy and pilot fish, Nikola Koljević, a Bosnian Serb who had taught in the United States and was an expert on Shakespeare. Koljević's specialty was sidling up to me after my meetings with Karadžić and portraying himself as the humane influence on Bosnian Serb policy. Several months after my departure from Belgrade, I saw a photograph of Koljević directing artillery fire on the civilian population of Sarajevo from a hill above the city.

Perhaps it was fitting that I should have one of my last meetings in doomed Yugoslavia with this macabre pair, the professor of English literature and the psychiatrist. At least Shakespeare and Freud would have understood the power of the irrational that provoked these and other madmen to destroy the human fabric of Yugoslavia.

Karadžić began the conversation by running down his usual litany of criticisms of the Europeans, attacks on Izetbegović's character and ideology, and laments that the United States should be so blind as to abandon its traditional Serbian allies. He then launched into a stream-of-consciousness justification for everything he was doing. "You have to understand Serbs, Mr. Zimmermann. They have been betrayed for centuries. Today they cannot live with other nations. They must have their own separate existence. They are a warrior race and they can trust only themselves to take by force what is their due. But this doesn't mean that Serbs can hate. Serbs are incapable of hatred."

I sought to pin him down. "What sort of Bosnian Serb republic do you have in mind?" I asked. "Will it be a part of Serbia?"

"That will be for the Bosnian Serb people to decide," he said. "But our first goal is independence, so we can live separately from others."

"Where will your capital be?" I asked.

"Why, Sarajevo, of course."

"But how can a city which is nearly 50 percent Muslim and only 30 percent Serb be the capital for the Serbs alone?"

Karadžić had a ready answer. "The city will be divided into Muslim, Serbian, and Croatian sections, so that no ethnic groups will have to live or work together."

"Just how will it be divided?"

"By walls," he said matter-of-factly. "Of course people will be able to pass from one part of the city to another, as long as they have permission and go through the checkpoints."

I thought of Sarajevo, which for centuries had been a moving symbol of the civility that comes from people of different ethnicities living in harmony. Then I thought of Berlin, where the wall, which had symbolized all the hatreds and divisions of the Cold War, had been torn down just over a year before.

"Do you mean," I asked, "that Sarajevo will be like Berlin before the wall was destroyed?"

"Yes," he answered, "our vision of Sarajevo is like Berlin when the wall was still standing."

Invitation To War

William Pfaff

THE MODERNITY OF ANCIENT HATREDS

WAR IN THE BALKANS is widely thought to be atavistic, the product of a perverse time warp that unloads fourteenth-century hatreds at the edge of the Europe of Maastricht, high-speed trains and the Single Market. Its cruelty is imputed to impulses beyond modern grasp or response. This is mystification by history.

The situation in Yugoslavia and Eastern Europe is the result of perfectly understandable forces and events of recent times: nineteenth-century romanticism, the emergence of the modern nation state after the French Revolution, the collapse of Hapsburg and Ottoman empires. Yugoslavia itself did not exist until 1918. Its supposedly primordial hatreds are a twentieth-century phenomenon.

The forces at work in contemporary ethnic war are neither ancient for the most part, nor incomprehensible. They are a modern affair, and a great deal could be done to contain their atrocious consequences. The most important step would be for NATO to guarantee against forcible change of those political frontiers in Eastern, East-Central and Balkan Europe that have not yet been violated but are threatened because of ethnic claims and rivalries. This guarantee would have to come from NATO, as the United Nations has lost its military credibility in the course of the Yugoslav affair. Such a guarantee would be politically difficult to organize but is militarily feasi-

WILLIAM PFAFF writes a syndicated column for the *International Herald Tribune*. His latest book, *The Wrath of Nations*, on nationalism, its origins and consequences, will be published in the fall.

ble. NATO is the true Great Power in Europe today. If this is not done, ethnic conflict risks dominating the course of events in the eastern half of Europe and the former Soviet Union for years to come, with serious jeopardy to the narrow but crucial gains that European (and Western) political civilization has made since 1945.

Already the sanctions broken in the Yugoslav war, the thresholds of law and international convention breached, the conventions of civilized political conduct violated, and the precedents of atrocity thus far set, have undermined that qualified confidence in the future of international relations that seemed to be justified by communism's collapse, political union in Europe, and the achievements of Western political cooperation. It was possible to believe that a new form of international order and cooperation might be extended eastward in Europe, eventually to incorporate the former Soviet Union itself. Instead, the assumption that atrocity is natural to the Balkans has rationalized the United States' and the West's acquiescence in aggressive war and their indirect collaboration in Yugoslavia's ethnic cleansing over the past two years. U.N. humanitarian interventions have in practice facilitated ethnic purge, and the Vance-Owen plan, meant to bring peace to Yugoslavia, would only ratify ethnic cleansing's outcome. New ethnic violence is thus invited elsewhere, outside the former Yugoslavia and inside Serbia itself, where the party that now holds 30 percent of the parliamentary seats demands the expulsion of all the Hungarians, Croatians, Slovenes, Muslim Albanians and Slovaks still inside Serbia's borders. More than 100,000 non-Serbs have already left the province of Vojvodina, largely populated by Hungarians. Hungary itself consequently risks becoming involved in the conflict, as does Albania, which is rightly concerned with the fate of the Muslim minority inside Serbia and Montenegro.

THE DELUSION OF ETHNIC PURITY

THE ETHNIC STATE is a product of the political imagination; it does not exist in reality. Ethnic nationalism is the product of a certain idea of the nation that originated in German romanticism and the German cultural and intellectual reaction to the universalizing ideas of the French Enlightenment and Revolution and other revolutionary wars. Romanticism glorified native earth, instinct, the priority of emotion over abstraction and thought, and hence the unity of "race" and state. It has, on the other hand, been the distinctive quality of the liberal democracies that they respect a principle of citizenship that is indifferent to "race." The two contemporary liberal states of which this is not true are Germany and Japan, and the drama of twentieth-century history for each has been closely connected to their traditional conceptions of themselves as racially exclusive. (Germany even now is altering its law of citizenship, in order to move away from the presumption that a German "race" exists.) Lord Acton, the great nineteenth-century liberal historian, wrote that by "attacking nationality in Russia, by delivering it in Italy, by governing in defiance of it in Germany and Spain," France's Revolutionary and Napoleonic armies had "called a new power into existence." Those conquered resisted the foreigner's rule, whatever his claim to be a liberator. "The protest against the domination of race over race ... grew into a condemnation of every state that included different races, and finally became the complete and consistent theory, that the state and the nation must be co-extensive." Thus did the ethnic state originate. The principle of universal national self-determination is, Acton concluded, "a retrograde step in history."

The idea of the ethnic nation is a permanent provocation to war.

No nation in Europe is ethnically pure. All are intermixtures of successive migrations of peoples. The nineteenth-century idea of the ethnic state was nonetheless made the basis of the First World War settlements in East-Central and Southeastern Europe and was enshrined in the U.N. Charter in 1945. The right to self-determination of the ethnic nation has been a principle of American foreign policy (if often observed in the breach) since 1917.

The ethnic definition of citizenship makes citizenship a matter of nature itself, of "race." Serbia's war to create a Greater Serbia is a logical application of the ethnic principle. All Serbs outside Serbia's borders have to be brought into a single state. Until then, the Serbian nation is persecuted and oppressed, threatened (to use the vocabulary current today in Belgrade) with "extermination." It equally follows from this principle that Hungarians outside Hungary cannot be allowed to rest until they are reunited with the Hungarians of Hungary proper—which is impossible other than at the expense of four other nations that consider the regions populated by these Hungarians as historically their own, and whose own populations in those regions would in some new, if hypothetical, "greater" Hungary naturally become in their turn national minorities (and no doubt irredentists).

The idea of the ethnic nation thus is a permanent provocation to war. It is an idea that makes spies and prospective insurgents of those who have the misfortune to live outside the shifting frontiers identified with their nationality, inviting their persecution by the people among whom they live, and rationalizing national expansion by the governments to which they are ethnically attached.

The ethnic state's contradictory and potentially catastrophic consequences manifested themselves in the 1930s, were suppressed by Stalin and by the Cold War, and now are liberated—if that is the word—by the Cold War's end. They are the reality of contemporary Southeastern Europe and the Soviet successor states. However, the international community is not helpless before the consequences of this idea. The West's passivity and incompetence in dealing with the Yugoslav crisis, hardly inevitable, has been the result of choices made by Western governments.

Yugoslavia's "ethnic war" is waged among three communities possessing no distinct physical characteristics or separate anthropological or "racial" origins. They are the same people. They have distinct histories, which is another matter. Moreover, these histories overlap; they are not exclusive. The notion of an exclusive, and exclusionary, ethnic existence for each of the Yugoslav peoples is an invention. Hungary is the principal state in southeastern Europe that can make a serious claim to be a "race." The Hungarians are a central Asian people who arrived in this region in the ninth century, and whose Finno-Ugric language is linked to Finnish and Estonian and has nothing to do with the languages of Hungary's neighbors.

The Albanians are a non-Slav people speaking an Indo-European language. The Romanians speak a Latin language dating from their incorporation into the Roman empire. Here and elsewhere the original populations have subsequently absorbed other migrant peoples: Goths, Huns, Avars and others. The Romanians' claim that they are a Roman nation, reemerging, as R. W. Seton-Watson put it, "after a thousand years of silence," requires the most serious qualification. Modern Macedonians are Slavs, not the Macedonians of antiquity—as the Greek government, which opposes Macedonia's recognition as "Macedonia," has recently gone to intemperate efforts to explain. The idea that the origins of modern Greece itself lie in Attic Greece is the invention of wishful Greek intellectuals in the nineteenth century and of romantic English Hellenophiles.

Yugoslavs, Czechs, Slovaks, modern Macedonians and Bulgarians, on the other hand, all are Slavic peoples, whose difference from the Poles, Russians, Ukrainians, etc., is largely a function of the period of their migration into the areas where they now live. The "South Slavs"—Serbs, Croatians and Bosnian Muslims—are all the same people, speaking the same language, although the Serbs write it in the Cyrillic alphabet and the Croatians in the Latin. They are physically indistinguishable. They became separated because in the early Middle Ages larger events put them into different historical camps, when Christianity divided between Rome and Constantinople over the momentous issue of the day: whether the Third Entity of the Holy Trinity "proceeded" or "went forth" from both Father and Son, as a phenomenon of love rather than generation, or from the Father alone, as the Eastern bishops seemed to defend. The Serbs found themselves under Byzantine jurisdiction and the Croats under that of Rome.

What today are the Bosnians were on the eastern side of this divide, and Bosnia's Muslims are generally thought to have at that time been believers in the Bogomil heresy, a dualism or Manicheanism that said that all material creation is evil, and which was linked to the Albigensian or Cathar heresy in southern France. When Bosnia-Herzegovina was overrun by the Muslim Turks in the fifteenth century, these Bogomils are presumed to have concluded that, as the Orthodox Church had persecuted them, it was safer to make allies of the Moslem conquerors, which was also a sound career move, placing them in the ruling camp. Orthodox Christianity survived chiefly in the countryside, among Serbian peasants, while the Islamic converts became prosperous and urbanized, as they have remained to the present day. There is a marked element of class war in today's "ethnic" war in Bosnia-Herzegovina.

A WAR OF HISTORIES AND VALUES

YUGOSLAVIA'S THEN is a war of histories, not ethnicity—unless, of course, the term ethnicity is considered to incorporate history as well, which would seem to rob it of its utility. But while each of the camps in today's war includes people who think they are avenging events from the fourteenth to the nineteenth centuries (from the battle of Kosovo to the Serbian military settlements' loss of privileges under Austrian rule), the political struggle between Serbs and Croatians is mainly an affair of the twentieth century, and their military conflict began only in 1941. There is no ancient and irrational conflict between them that exempts them from responsibility for their actions or from accountability to the norms of modern international law.

Since their liberation from the Ottoman Empire early in the nineteenth century, the Serbs have tried to unite the South Slavs, claiming primacy among them as the largest of them and the first to win modern independence. However, the Serb minority inside Hapsburg Hungary cooperated politically with the Croatians until the collapse of the Austro-Hungarian Empire. Then, in 1917, Serbia was chiefly responsible for the creation of Yugoslavia, the Kingdom of the South Slavs, under a Serbian monarch. The French historian of Yugoslavia, Paul Garde, says,

> The first real manifestation of hostility dates from 1902, when the Serbs, proud of the renaissance of their people, began to contest the separate existence of a distinct Croatian nation, and a Serbian journalist in Zagreb, Nikola Stojanovic, published an article with the provocative title, 'Either Your Destruction or Ours,' which caused anti-Serbian riots. Nevertheless ... the gulf did not really open until 1918, when to their mutual unhappiness, the two

> people were united in a single state, the Yugoslav monarchy, where one of them, the Serbs, exercised an absolute domination, and the other was treated as a negligible entity. All the rest has come from that.[1]

The struggle in Yugoslavia has today also become a war of political values, which is the particular reason why it is of importance to the future of neighboring regions. The government of Bosnia-Herzegovina in Sarajevo is formally committed to the principles of the nonethnic, secular democratic state, in which all of the communities of the former Yugoslavia could continue to live in association, as they did under Tito. The Bosnian people have, as the novelist Miroslav Karaulac bitterly remarks, "acquired the fatal habit of living together, a quality which the various armies now fighting one another are, by means of a bloodbath, attempting to correct."

The Serbian nationalists who are chiefly, although by no means exclusively, responsible for the war, deny the possibility of living together, insisting that historical fatality makes coexistence impossible. Yet coexistence was the reality of Yugoslavia from 1917 until 1991, with the exception of the four Second World War years, which saw a genocidal assault upon the Serbs by Croatia's fascist collaborationist wartime government—one cause of the atrocities practiced by Serbs in recent months. The Serbian nationalists and irredentists have spent the past 18 months working to turn their assertion of the impossibility of coexistence into fact, and for practical purposes have now undoubtedly succeeded. Hannah Arendt observed 50 years ago in connection with Stalinism and Nazism that it is quite possible, through lies accompanied by violence, to manufacture fact.

THE DANGERS OF TIMIDITY

THE RESPONSE of the international community to the Yugoslav war has been a timid and unsuccessful effort to find a negotiated solution while halting the fighting and atrocities. In the course of this, the U.N. Security Council and the European Community have for practical purposes accepted the results of Serbian and Croatian aggres-

[1] *Le Monde*, Aug. 18, 1992.

sion and "ethnic cleansing" as faits accomplis. The International Court of Justice at The Hague, the highest instance of international law, has declined to accept the Bosnian government's complaint of international aggression. The United Nations and the European Community have proposed to enforce Bosnia-Herzegovina's ethnic partition by means of a reinforced military intervention to impose observance of the Vance-Owen plan—should that plan ever actually be accepted.

The international significance of these policies lies chiefly in the influence they will have upon the other territorially irreconcilable ethnic claims being made elsewhere. Tension exists between Hungary and several of its neighbors with Hungarian minorities. Hungary's present borders are those of the Treaty of Trianon of 1920, which partitioned Austria-Hungary in order to create the new ethnic states of Czechoslovakia and Yugoslavia, and to reward Romania for having fought on the Allied side in the First World War—as well as for having invaded Hungary in 1919 to overthrow the communist seizure of power there, led by Béla Kun.

The Vance-Owen plan could only intensify insecurities and perpetuate national revanchism.

There were, until recent events in Vojvodina, 350,000 Hungarians inside Serbia, two million in Romania, 600,000 in Slovakia, and 170,000 in Ukraine. The Hungarians in Serbia now experience the apparent overture to active ethnic cleansing. There are serious difficulties between Hungarians in Romanian Transylvania and the Romanian authorities, particularly those at the local level. Hungary's concern to defend these Hungarians abroad is usually interpreted in the other countries as a potential threat to their territorial integrity. This can scarcely be thought surprising when the Prime Minister of Hungary, Jozsef Antall, a Christian Democrat with the reputation and record of a moderate, claims that he is "prime minister in the soul of fifteen million Hungarians"—there being only 10.5 million Hungarians inside Hungary. In January the Hungarian minister of defense, Lajos Für, declared that "fifteen million Hungarians have their eyes fixed on us. We must prove ourselves worthy of this historic challenge."

The implication is that the Hungarians of Romanian Transylvania, of Vojvodina in Serbia, and those in southern Slovakia and Ukraine are not unqualifiedly the citizens of the countries in which they live, but "in their soul" give their allegiance to the prime minister of Hungary. Equally implicit in the Hungarian officials' statements is that someday Hungary will have to do something about this situation of Hungarians abroad. The Hungarians have refused thus far to include an engagement of mutual respect for the existing frontier in a projected new treaty with Romania. The danger in all of this is obvious. There is serious risk in the deteriorating and persecuted condition of the Albanian majority in the province of Kosovo in Serbia, and in Sanjak, near Montenegro, provoking instability on the Albanian and Macedonian borders of the new, truncated Yugoslavia, with Greece, Bulgaria and Turkey all interested parties.

Any new attempt to find solutions based on the principle of ethnic self-determination is likely to prove as vain, if not destructive, as it has been in the past. The insecurity of ethnic minorities and majorities cannot be eliminated by redrafting maps, as in the Vance-Owen plan, since no map can satisfactorily separate the nationalities of the region and satisfy their ambitions and historical claims. These are the reasons why the Vance-Owen plan could only intensify insecurities and perpetuate the intellectual, political and moral corruption of national revanchism and ethnic revindication. No attempt to rework the territorial divisions of the region on ethnic lines or to put minorities under U.N. protection can be expected to work other than through internationally imposed population transfers of an utterly unacceptable scale and nature.

The Vance-Owen plan would not even make peace in Bosnia, since the Bosnian Serbs consider themselves cheated by its terms, and remain determined eventually to link the newly designated Serbian cantons with Serbia proper, so as to create a Greater Serbia. The other communities rightly regard themselves victimized by the Serbs and will await their opportunity for revenge. It is at best a plan for an armistice, during which the United Nations will attempt to protect the Bosnian Serbs against their victims, and at the same time prevent them from extending their holdings. This military assignment is far more daunting and open-ended than a direct military intervention to halt the aggression would have been two years ago, or even in summer 1992. A military intervention to impose the Vance-Owen settlement upon a population that is virtually unanimous in rejecting it is a task without practical limits or a reasonable prospect of success.

THE SANCTITY OF BORDERS

SMALL WARS in the Balkans do not directly threaten the West's security today because Great Power Europe is not, as it was in 1914, a tinderbox awaiting a light. The danger that comes from successful aggression and ethnic purge in Yugoslavia is primarily moral and political, since these events contradict the reign of order and legality produced in Western Europe, and among the democracies as a whole, since the end of the Second World War. An effective international guarantee of existing frontiers in the Balkans and Eastern Europe, so as to deprive transnational ethnic rivalry of its political and military explosiveness, could provide one substantial form of defense against the spread of violence and disorder. Such a guarantee would undoubtedly have to be implemented by NATO, itself a model of multinational cooperation among nations whose history until 1945 was of hatreds and war. This guarantee would give the governments of Eastern Europe the assurance, warning and relief of knowing that the Western powers have collectively undertaken to prevent any new frontier change in the region that has not been peacefully negotiated by the interested parties and condoned by international consensus.

The guarantee would have to be credible. Any violation or threat to a frontier should produce a NATO deployment in the threatened country in support of its territorial defense. The NATO force must be given a mandate to fight if necessary. There would also have to be diplomatic intervention and generally a more activist and interventionist Western policy in defense of national minority rights in Eastern Europe and the Balkans. The precedents and legal basis for this already exist in the institutions of the Conference for Security and Cooperation in Europe and the Council of Europe. They are not yet effectively used.

It is a policy on which agreement seems achievable, reuniting the Western powers divided by the Yugoslav tragedy, by giving them a common positive program. It is capable of recovering for the West moral as well as political ground lost by their fiasco in Yugoslavia. It could lay a base of stability for the construction in Eastern Europe of interstate relations of security and confidence, freed of the threat of transnational ethnic claims, offering the possibility for a peaceful clarification and improvement of the status of ethnic minorities, and perhaps opening the way to an eventual mutual security arrangement among the East European governments themselves, possibly in a new association with NATO.

One speaks of such a new association with reference to Southeastern and Eastern Europe alone, and not the Soviet successor states, because political realism, a sense of what is attainable, so dictates. The ethnic conflicts of the ex-Soviet states are beyond the competence of the Western powers to influence constructively (rather than destructively), and for the most part are beyond their practical reach. The West effectively has already decided to make no attempt to interfere in conflicts in the ex-Soviet Confederation of Independent States, other than, probably, the case of an attempt by Russia to reincorporate the Baltic nations. There is little the West can actually do about the outcome of struggles between Azeris and Armenians, Tajik Muslims and National Communists, the peoples of Ingushetia and Northern Ossetia, and those of Southern Ossetia and Georgians. These also may reasonably, if cruelly, be judged to be of slight consequence to the West, except as they may destabilize Russia's recovery.

The Balkan and East European situations are different. An enlarged Balkan war, potentially involving Greece and Turkey, both NATO members, or Hungary, a candidate for European Community membership, or Bulgaria, could not be without serious consequences for Germany, Austria, Slovakia, the Czech Republic and Russia, which has historical and emotional links to Bulgaria and Serbia—therefore affecting the security of the United States as well.

THE MORAL PRECEDENT

NOTHING RATIONALIZES the horrors inflicted on and by the peoples of former Yugoslavia during the past 18 months. Certainly history does not justify them. These atrocities have been possible only by a deliberate submission by the individuals involved to a collective nihilism of essentially ideological origin. This fact is apparent in the chronic drunkenness of militiamen who live with the knowledge that they have murdered and raped their neighbors and friends. It is evident in the lies coolly spoken by the Bosnian Serb physicians and university professors who, from their headquarters in the hills over Sarajevo, direct their campaign of ethnic purification. For all of them the passage to a radiant future (or a radiant past, as it has been better put) passes through a darkened tunnel of repudiation of what they have been until now, as citizens of the Yugoslav state that existed since 1918 and as professionals and intellectuals, men and women. They are deep in this tunnel now, and many are frightened to emerge. It is visible in their faces.

The same thing can certainly happen elsewhere, as it has happened before—and not that long ago. The West has managed to survive the totalitarian experience and the horrors then committed, constructing a novel community of liberal states that has seemed to contain in it a promise of expansion from its Atlantic and West European core, so as to bring other states into a moral as well as political community in which war has been ruled out as an agency of national interest. What has gone on in Yugoslavia constitutes a savage challenge to this order. If events in Yugoslavia are allowed to set the precedent for the conduct of other peoples caught up in the passionate fictions of ethnicity, the consequences will be very bad for everyone. This does not have to be so. But there is little evidence yet of a Western willingness to do the practical things that might prevent so dark an outcome.

How to Defeat Serbia

David Gompert

FIGHT FOR A PRINCIPLED PEACE

THOSE WHOSE SOLE concern has been to keep the United States out of the Yugoslav conflict may view American policy over the past four years as successful. The rest of us—even those who had a hand in that policy—know failure when we see it. True, the war has not spread beyond Croatia and Bosnia, owing in part to an American containment strategy. Also true, the human agony would have been worse had the United States not supported an international relief effort that deserves more praise than it gets. Yet we cannot evade the larger truth: the United States promised to stay in Europe after the Cold War in order to help keep peace and sustain the democratic revolution; but a war of aggression has been waged and won by a most undemocratic regime. The United States proclaimed principles of peaceful change for a new era; but those principles have been wantonly disregarded. We said "never again"; but again the intolerable has happened in Europe.

Great as our sorrow is for the slaughter and for our mistakes, it is unfair to suggest that the United States bears the main responsibility. Our military superiority and international leadership role do not obligate us to sacrifice our sons and daughters to combat brutality wherever it occurs. Moreover, the lack of a purposeful effort by our European allies to prevent or stop a vicious conflict on their conti-

---

DAVID GOMPERT is a Vice President at RAND and former Senior Director for Europe and Eurasia on the Bush administration's National Security Council staff.

PHOTOGRAPH BY STEVE LEHMAN, SABA

Can these men be stopped?

nent not only surpasses American shortcomings but has hamstrung U.S. policy. Still, we must see that American interests and values, its credibility and self-respect have been damaged in the former Yugoslavia, and we must thus recognize the face of failure.

The United States is not destined to keep failing in the Balkans. Rather, it can devise a strategy that responds to the fact of Serbia's military success and, from here on, both protects American interests and repairs its principles. The Clinton administration has established some limits of what will be tolerated, and it has created the possibility of a continued, if tenuous, Bosnian state. But there is a danger of misinterpreting and thus misplaying this opportunity. A strategy aimed at achieving an early, final settlement through a combination of sticks (limited air strikes) and carrots (relaxation of sanctions) would be a mistake, whether or not it succeeded, leading either to a futile escalation or to the codification of Serbian conquests in an unstable peace agreement enforced by U.S. troops. Yet wide and relentless NATO bombing at a level that could turn the tide of war or extract sweeping concessions from the Serbs would require a radical, and unrealistic, shift in Western and U.N. attitudes. The best alternative is to conduct a cold war against Serbia—one of indefinite duration but certain outcome—while in the meantime using NATO's military power more effectively to ensure that relief reaches Bosnia's innocent victims.

ANTICIPATING CHAOS

CONTRARY TO A WIDELY held view, the Bush administration was well aware of the dangers in Yugoslavia prior to the crisis. It simply knew of no way to prevent a violent disintegration. National Security Adviser Brent Scowcroft and Deputy Secretary of State Lawrence Eagleburger, among others, understood Yugoslavia and its volcanic nature. There was no "intelligence failure," no inattention due to preoccupation with the collapse of communism or Iraq's invasion of Kuwait. Rather, despite considerable deliberation and diplomatic action, no good option emerged to arrest the accelerating, awful logic of breakup and war. Serbs were usurping power in Belgrade; Slovenes were determined to be free from the Serbs; Croats were destined to follow the Slovenes; Serbs, in turn, were dead set against living as a minority in an independent Croatia; and the Bosnian powder keg was set to explode once the fuse was lit in Croatia.

By 1990 Washington was pessimistic but not paralyzed. It supported the teetering Yugoslav federal government of Ante Marković, who was committed to democracy and a market economy. The Bush administration also pressed Serbian strongman Slobodan Milošević to stop his oppression of Albanians in Kosovo and his illegal seizure of Yugoslav federal assets and authority, which were fueling Slovenian and Croatian secessionism. At the same time, the Slovenes and Croats were urged to consider arrangements short of dissolution. None of these American efforts was fruitful.

U.S. policy was motivated by a judgment that a peaceful breakup was infeasible.

While the identity of the archvillain—Milošević , Inc.—was never in doubt, the Bush administration had scant sympathy for Slovene and Croat separatists. The former seemed willing to trigger a Yugoslav war so long as they could escape both Yugoslavia and the war. The Croatian regime, hardly democratic, adopted policies regarding minorities that stoked fears among Serbs living in Croatia of a revival of the Ustashe, the infamous Nazi-style secret police who butchered Serbs during World War II. American policymakers thus saw cynicism behind the declared "right" of Slovene and Croat nationalists to be free, democratic and part of the (Roman Catholic) West, even as these same U.S. policymakers knew that Milošević's power-grabbing was the main force propelling Yugoslavia toward a violent end.

U.S. policy prior to hostilities was not motivated by an attachment to a unified Yugoslavia but by a judgment, which proved all too correct, that a peaceful breakup was infeasible. American strategic interest in the integrity of Yugoslavia, per se, ended with the collapse of the Soviet threat to Europe. By late 1990 the overriding U.S. concern about Yugoslavia was to avert a Balkan war. Washington believed that a disintegration of Yugoslavia was bound to be violent because Serbs would sooner fight than accept minority status in an independent

Croatia; that the fighting would engulf much of Yugoslavia, because the urge of each republic to secede would grow as others seceded; and that the human toll would be terrible, because Yugoslavia was seething with both weapons and latent hate-fear. (The grisly particulars—detention camps, ethnic cleansing, mass rapes, shelling of civilian populations—were not predicted, though perhaps they could have been.) Those who criticize the Bush administration for contributing to the outbreak of the conflict by favoring unity have yet to explain how favoring disunity would have prevented the conflict.

As the crisis deepened, the United States advanced several sound principles: Yugoslavia should become democratic throughout; borders, external and internal alike, should be altered only by mutual consent, not unilaterally or by force; Yugoslavia should not be held together by force; members of minority groups throughout Yugoslavia should have the same rights as all other individuals. That every one of these principles was thoroughly trashed within a year underscores the scale of the U.S. failure but does not invalidate the norms on which they are based. (It is worth noting that essentially these same principles were observed, more or less, in the breakup of Czechoslovakia, where not a shot was fired.)

Knowing that disintegration meant a savage war, the United States favored transforming Yugoslavia into a confederation of quasi-sovereign states. Such an arrangement was also urged by the leaders of Macedonia and Bosnia-Herzegovina, who saw great peril in complete dissolution. Washington hoped that a loose structure would satisfy the Slovenes (and thus the Croats) while also convincing the Serbs that it was the only way to hold Yugoslavia together. Indeed, moderate Slovenes and Croats favored such an outcome and welcomed this American stance, knowing as they did that secession would lead to bloodshed. U.S. strategy, which culminated in Secretary of State James Baker's mid-1991 visit to Yugoslavia, sought to persuade the Slovenes to postpone unilateral separation, while demanding (toothlessly) that Milošević adhere to the constitution and warning the leadership of the Serb-dominated Yugoslav National Army (JNA) not to use force to save Yugoslavia.

But the Slovenes proved indifferent to the fatal consequences for others of their actions. They seceded and took the Croats with them. In response, the JNA declared itself obligated to act in defense of the union and its own military assets. Serbs living in Croatia took up arms without delay. The Baker mission failed, but the secretary gave no "green light" to the Serbs to use force to preserve Yugoslav unity. Had the U.S. championed Slovenian and Croatian secession instead of urging restraint, the results would hardly have been better.

'THE HOUR OF EUROPE'

AMERICAN RELIANCE on its European partners to take the lead in Yugoslavia proved to be a grave mistake that compounded the West's failure. Before the fighting began, the United States urged the European Community to accept leadership out of a belief that the allies had more leverage than the United States to head off a catastrophe. American attempts in 1990 to get the Europeans to face the dangers were brushed aside: an American proposal to consult in NATO was declined, with the French accusing the United States of "overdramatizing" the problem. Not until 1991 was the EC seized with the risks of Serbian policies and Slovenian secession. The $4 billion aid carrot the EC then produced could have been the last hope for avoiding war, had it not been dangled in front of the Yugoslavs at least a year too late.

At the highest levels and at every turn, the United States encouraged the allies to engage and offered its support. The Europeans favored EC leadership because Yugoslavia was viewed as an opportune foreign policy challenge at the very moment German Chancellor Helmut Kohl, French President François Mitterrand and others wished to display the EC's ability to act effectively and cohesively. Luxembourg's foreign minister, speaking for the EC's troika of emissaries, proclaimed it "the hour of Europe," a quote whose painful echo is a reminder of how badly the Europeans misjudged the dogs of this Balkan war. The United States deferred to the Europeans' wish that transatlantic coordination take place in EC-U.S. channels instead of in NATO. The alliance was thus kept out of the crisis until it became clear that the Bosnian conflict exceeded the capacities of all other international institutions.

Broadly speaking, U.S. handling of the Yugoslav crisis, at least from 1990 through 1992, contradicted and undermined its declared policy regarding the centrality and purpose of NATO in post-Cold War Europe. During that period, the Bush administration insisted that America's role in European security would be maintained despite the disappearance of the Soviet threat and that NATO was the keystone of European security and the proper venue for crisis management. The administration informed Congress that a residual American presence in Europe on the order of 150,000 troops was needed to preserve stability and peace. The Rome summit at the end of 1991 endorsed NATO's new role and revised alliance military strategy to emphasize force projection over territorial defense.[1]

Yet the Bush administration did not press for the use of NATO to set and manage Western strategy, much less to intervene, owing to a combination of the EC's desire to lead and its own concern that NATO involvement would shift responsibility to the United States. Washington wanted the EC to succeed, but the clearer it became that the EC could not, the less eager the United States was to see the alliance, and thus itself, saddled with a no-win problem. Predictably, the attempt to hold the Yugoslavia crisis at arm's length did not spare the United States the effects of, or responsibility for, the failure that followed.

As fighting intensified in Croatia in late 1991, the United States was hesitant to recognize the two breakaway republics. This hesitation stemmed from a conviction, also held by U.N. envoy Cyrus Vance, that premature recognition would scuttle Vance's effort to obtain a ceasefire and deploy a peacekeeping force in Croatia. There was also a reluctance to recognize Croatia and Slovenia before recognizing Bosnia-Herzegovina. Both U.S. policy and the EC's Arbitration Commission held that recognition of Bosnia should await the outcome of a referendum there. When a two-thirds majority of Bosnians—made up of Muslims and Croats, with Bosnia's Serbs boycotting—voted for inde-

[1] Ironically, although NATO did not have in mind the possible use of its new "rapid reaction corps," the JNA was not so sure. The Yugoslav defense minister, General Veljko Kadijevic, told me after the Rome summit that he suspected the alliance of preparing an intervention force.

pendence, the United States pressured the EC to recognize Bosnia in exchange for U.S. recognition of Slovenia and Croatia. Recognition of Bosnia did not precipitate the use of force by the Bosnian Serbs any more than it deterred it. Very simply, Bosnian Muslims would not stay in a rump Yugoslavia dominated by Serbia, and Bosnian Serbs would not stay in a Bosnia dominated by Muslims. In any case, there was no legal basis for the United States to recognize Croatia but not Bosnia-Herzegovina.

The West was divided and immobilized in the crucial period between the EC's recognition of Slovenia and Croatia in December 1991 and the European-American agreement in March 1992 that Slovenia, Croatia and Bosnia should all be recognized. Bowing to right-wing and Croat expatriate pressure, German leaders muscled their EC colleagues into recognizing Slovenia and Croatia against the better judgment of the United States, the United Nations and indeed most EC foreign ministries. In doing so, Bonn hastened Bosnian secession and a war from which Germany, due to its history and constitutional restraints, could remain aloof while its partners faced risk and sacrifice. The Germans favored standing up to the Serbs, knowing that the responsibility would fall to others.

European governments did not seem to grasp the huge danger in Bosnia.

Consumed by their dispute over recognition, the Western powers failed utterly to prepare for the conflict in Bosnia they had every reason to expect. They failed even to call for the prompt departure of the JNA from the newly recognized country. Worse, the opportunity was lost to dispatch to Bosnia a peacekeeping force to discourage violence before it began. Because the U.N. force in Croatia was already shaping up as a major burden, there was no enthusiasm in the West or the United Nations for a significant new commitment. The EC was and would remain inert. Even on the eve of disaster, European governments did not seem to grasp the huge danger in Bosnia. At the same time, the Bush administration was hardening its resolve to keep U.S. troops out of Yugoslavia altogether. So the West watched Bosnia slide into unspeakable violence.

TURNING HELPERS INTO HOSTAGES

THE LONDON CONFERENCE of August 1992 was a lost opportunity, a turning point and a sorry chapter in Western mishandling of the conflict. The conference, attended by an accommodating Californian, Milan Panić, as premier of the new "Yugoslavia," produced a package of useful concrete agreements among the parties. If honored, these measures would have curtailed the fighting, ended atrocities, guaranteed safe and effective humanitarian relief and set the stage for political negotiations.

In the days and weeks that followed, however, the Serbs willfully ignored every accord reached and commitment made. This affront drew no response from the West or the U.N. Security Council. The United States was disinclined to use air power to enforce the various London agreements, in part because of the perceived risk of being drawn in and in part because of the particular difficulty of air-policing restrictions on artillery. The British reinforced American hesitation by insisting that they would participate in the U.N. Protective Force (UNPROFOR) only if the United States did not introduce air power, lest it anger the Serbs.

The Europeans were also adamant about the need to maintain the arms embargo on the Muslims. Until its final days, the Bush administration shared this reluctance to arm the Muslims, despite the Serbs' failure to abide by the London accords. Its analysis showed that lifting the embargo would increase Muslim casualties and the suffering of innocents, impair humanitarian relief and bring no change in the military fortunes of the parties. This fear of fueling the conflict to no avail outweighed the view that only the government in Sarajevo had the right to decide whether to accept the risks inherent in defending Bosnia and its people. When President Bush, feeling strong Arab pressure, reversed his position on the arms embargo before leaving office, London and Paris blocked the change, showing once again that the presence of Europeans (and absence of Americans) in UNPROFOR has given the allies a veto over U.S. action, just as it has given the Serbs a veto over Western action.

Western inaction after London told the Serbs in unmistakable terms that there would be no intervention. The Serbs were further emboldened as it became clear that the British and French considered their UNPROFOR contingents virtual hostages and therefore sought to avoid provocation. Concerned about the dangerous precedent of bowing to threats against blue helmets, the United States offered in late 1992 to use air power against the Serbs if they harmed U.N. personnel. The United Kingdom declined the offer; indeed, London's repeated public display of concern for the safety of its UNPROFOR contingent encouraged the Serbs to threaten these and other U.N. forces as a way to derail Western attempts to interfere with their ethnic cleansing of Muslims. Other blue helmets in other nasty circumstances in the future might wish that the West had shown more grit in Bosnia.

KUWAIT OR VIETNAM?

PRESIDENT BUSH'S DECISION not to allow American ground forces to play any role under any circumstances in Bosnia effectively precluded large-scale Western military intervention. The president's advisers knew that Western military intervention in Bosnia really meant American military intervention with token allied forces, owing to the allies' lack of serious intervention capabilities. The administration also feared that introducing any U.S. ground forces, even to escort humanitarian relief convoys, could lead to a creeping, eventually massive U.S. engagement since the United States and only the United States would be under pressure to escalate its involvement to ensure success. Involvement in Bosnia was viewed as more akin to Vietnam than to Desert Storm. Notwithstanding public outcry over televised Bosnian horrors, the Bush administration was convinced that the American public, seeing no vital interests at stake, would not support the level of commitment and casualties that might be required to succeed. Events since (e.g., Somalia) suggest that this reading was politically accurate.

Other uses of force, such as striking Serbian artillery in range of population centers, were rejected as militarily ineffective, as well as the first foot on the proverbial slippery slope. The Bush administration—no rookie when it came to using force—was not prepared to threaten force unless it was willing and able to execute not only the specific threat but whatever steps beyond might be needed to prevail. Panama and Kuwait were held up as evidence of the merits of acting only with "decisive force"; even administration hawks knew that Bosnia would be more difficult to manage militarily and politically. Nor was the president inclined to gamble that the Serbs would lose their nerve when confronted with American might. While likely Serb reactions to U.S. strikes were pure guesswork, the Bush administration believed the consequences of guessing wrong were prohibitive, in the sense that once committed the United States would then have to use all necessary force to avoid failure, despite the absence of vital stakes and firm public support.

CLINTON COMPOUNDS THE CONFUSION

THE "LIFT AND STRIKE" initiative of February 1993 accentuated transatlantic discord, highlighted irremediable defects in the Vance-Owen plan, demonstrated the U.S. inability to lead, raised Muslim hopes that Western intervention would occur after all, and committed the United States to join in the enforcement of a dubious peace agreement. Perversely, it signaled to the Serbs that a large NATO force would be inserted in Bosnia not if the fighting continued, but only if it stopped. Not surprisingly, the new administration soon retreated to the same public posture that its predecessor employed when stymied, wrongly portraying the Bosnian conflict as a hopelessly complicated civil war, with all parties at fault and no American interests at stake.

There rested American policy, uneasily, until a Serbian mortar shell hit Sarajevo's crowded marketplace—an obscene act, but one no worse than other atrocities routinely committed in Bosnia. Western television footage was gruesome enough to prompt Washington to insist on a NATO ultimatum threatening air strikes if the Serbs failed to pull their heavy weapons out of range of Sarajevo. When the threat worked, American advocates of air strikes proclaimed that they had been right all along to challenge the view that hitting the Serbs would simply get their backs up and endanger U.N. peacekeepers on the ground. But within a few weeks, defiant Serbs were shelling the "safe" city of Gorazde, firing on NATO aircraft and detaining U.N. peacekeepers, thus casting doubt on Pavlovian explanations of Serbian behavior. In the end, the Serbs edged away from Gorazde. But overall, it appears that spotty use of NATO military power will have spotty results. Yes, force impresses the Serbs more than other forms of coercion; but doses of force too small to alter military outcomes may not impress them enough to alter their behavior strategically.

The United States and its allies are right, at last, to use force when U.N. Security Council decisions or commitments made by the Serbs themselves are flouted, when U.N. personnel are threatened, or when humanitarian operations are hindered. However, since Western governments, reflecting public sentiment, have no intention of intervening decisively in Bosnia, there is little chance that air strikes, here and there, against Bosnian Serb tanks and artillery pieces will change the course of the war or bring about a principled and enduring peace. Thus, Serbian military gains to date will not be contested, and any formal settlement available at this time is therefore bound to reward aggression.

AT ROOT, A EUROPEAN FAILURE

IT IS WORTH ASKING how U.S. policy over the past four years could have been such a dismal failure. Consistent U.S. leadership might have made a difference. Why was it not forthcoming from the seasoned, interventionist, Atlanticist Bush administration—from the folks who built the coalition and sent the force that crushed Iraq? This was not a case of a breakdown of Washington's ability to read and act on the warning signs. Rather, George Bush and his lieutenants studied the facts and concluded that leadership in this crisis would have had major drawbacks for the United States.

Following the Gulf War, a leading role in Yugoslavia would have implied that the United States could and would act as international policeman, even in an area of more immediate importance to America's rich European partners. Moreover, this was a problem with no good, feasible solutions. Only massive Western intervention would have stopped and reversed Serbian aggression, not some smart bomb down the right Serbian chimney. The United States faced by far the largest risks because it had (and has) the only real intervention capability. And the larger the task, the greater the American burden and casualties, and the greater the need for resolute public support. Yet Desert Storm taught the American people, wrongly, that vital interests could be defended with a handful of casualties in a video-game war. Popular backing for the use of force in Yugoslavia, ambivalent at the outset, would quickly evaporate. Lacking solutions, the United States had no reason to wrest leadership from the eager Europeans.

Any formal settlement available at this time is bound to reward aggression.

Neither the United States nor any other power saw its vital interests imperiled by the conflict. The West had a political and moral interest in humanitarian relief and a strategic interest in containment—and in fact the United States and EC have been successful in protecting those two interests. (The terse Christmas Day warning from Bush to Miloševič in 1992 that Serbian violence against the Albanians of Kosovo would expose Serbia to attack may well have prevented conflict there.) But Western leaders did not see—or, if they saw, did not translate into public support and purposeful policies—that the crisis, in Bosnia especially, was setting the worst possible precedents for the new era. They did not appreciate the importance of defeating this case of fiendish nationalism before it metastasized elsewhere in the former communist world.

At the root of American failure was West European failure. Had the Europeans confronted the problem when the United States alerted them, had they acted more cohesively, had they been more willing to sacrifice, the United States could have joined them in a better, if not entirely successful, strategy. Under both administrations, the United States has been prepared to do more, including use force, but not instead of or over the objections of its allies. Although many British, French, Dutch, Spanish and other European men and women have served courageously in the Yugoslav conflict, Europe itself has been a flop. That each of the most powerful members of the EC had its own agenda not only helped ensure EC failure but reminds us why Europeans, left to themselves, tend to mismanage Europe's security.

Finally, poor as Western policy has been, we should not forget that Yugoslavs destroyed their multiethnic state, caused the ensuing war and fought it in a most heinous way. The Slovenes acted unilaterally without regard for what they knew would be tragic consequences for others; the Croats gave ethnic Serbs every reason to fear for their safety; Milošević drew to the surface and then retailed the venom of ethnic hatred that had been inactive in modern Yugoslavia. The abundance of Balkan villains and absence of innocents—except for the people—do not excuse Western failures yet help explain why it was and remains so difficult to find solutions.

FREEZE OUT THE SERBS

BELGRADE WANTS A political settlement that will secure Serbian conquests, end economic sanctions and open the way to creation of Greater Serbia. The West, especially Western Europe, wants a settlement to end the violence but realizes that Serbian territorial concessions will be necessary. The United States is not prepared to carry out the kind of heavy bombing campaign that could change the calculus fundamentally, and even if it were, the Europeans, Russians and U.N. relief authorities would block it. But the allies are prepared to negotiate away the economic sanctions on Serbia. Thus eagerness in the West to stop the fighting could present Milošević with the opportunity to become victor, peacemaker and father of Greater Serbia.

If the United States goes along, and agrees to pressure the Muslims to yield, there is a good chance of getting a bad peace—a settlement devoid of principle; an outcome that would strengthen a regional bully whose creed and conduct are the opposite of what the United States wants to foster in the former communist world; a formal acceptance of the results of aggression and ethnic cleansing; a deal obtained by forgoing further punishment of the aggressors; an unstable peace. Are we now condemned to add to our failures by codifying their consequences? Is this a solution we want American soldiers to enforce?

There is a less bad future, provided the United States is prepared to play a long game. A sustained economic and information war against Serbia should in time topple the Belgrade regime and permit a more principled and lasting settlement in Yugoslavia than anything within reach today. So far, sanctions have not brought down Milošević nor changed Serbian policies. But in time, industrial demise and wretched living conditions should create pressure for change. Such a development would be no more astonishing than what has occurred in the past five years in most of the communist world, the Middle East and South Africa. Years—decades, if need be—of deprivation, isolation and misery should produce a democratic revolution and leaders eager to earn a place for the Serbs in the society of nations. Is that not a better time for a final settlement? Instead of rushing toward a bad agreement that will give this abominable regime the chance to recover and look respectable, we should commit to quarantine Serbia until the virus it carries has been eradicated.

Is this realistic? Even now, there are concerns that the sanctions regime will not hold. But a patient cold war against Serbia would not require that sanctions be airtight, provided they are durable. It is a mistake to expect sanctions swiftly to choke out the life of a regime as hardy and resourceful as that of Milošević, backed by the legendary Serb patriotism he is able to sustain with his information machine. A better model might be the slow death of the economies of the Soviet Union and Eastern Europe, leading to the revolutions of 1989-91. In Serbia's case, the process can be nudged along by a broader, if still imperfect, denial of the benefits of foreign trade.

Would the allies see it through? West European allies have proved quite stout in sticking with sanctions against South Africa, Libya and Iraq, as well as with restrictions on economic intercourse with the U.S.S.R. Why in the case of Serbia should they not be able to endure the limited effects on themselves? And if the Europeans believe sanctions cannot be sustained, why do they believe the Serbs will make important concessions to get them removed? In any case, even leaky sanctions should not be lifted in a trade for a flawed and unstable peace settlement. In sum, the allies have a weak case for ending Serbia's economic isolation in return for a bad settlement, and a firm U.S. stance should prevail, especially since the Europeans cannot easily capitulate without American consent.

A more legitimate concern is with the harmful effect of the embargo on the frail new democracies of southeast Europe: Albania, Macedonia, Bulgaria and Romania. The West cannot treat them as expendable. Instead, the EC and the United States should expand and sustain economic support so that these frontline states can survive and succeed as Serbia falters. Supporting struggling societies recently liberated from communism is a worthy cause in any case. It has done much for the Poles, Hungarians and Czechs. The cost has been affordable, and the results are promising. And, of course, the West would not be helping the Balkan democracies in the long run by ending Serbia's isolation and letting Milošević emerge as the victorious leader of a menacing local power.

Sustained economic and information warfare should topple the Belgrade regime.

Economic progress among Serbia's neighbors could accentuate the political effects of Serbia's own economic decline, provided its citizens are informed about the reasons for and consequences of their leper status. To date, Serbs may be miserable, but they believe they are right, and they blame the West, not Milošević, for their plight. But therein lies a source of hope for the long-term strategy suggested here. The information revolution had as much to do with the collapse of Soviet communism as did the rot within. Today the majority of Serbs believe what they see and hear on the television station controlled by Milošević. Tomorrow—certainly within a few years—Milošević should be unable to prevent them from learning the truth, about him, about Bosnia, about the atrocities, about the reasons for their hardship, about their options.

This natural development could stand a boost. The Western democracies have done far less than their technology permits to challenge Milošević's information monopoly. Television is the key but not the only medium that needs to be developed and exploited. Fax networks riddled and wrecked the Soviet system, and the Serbian regime is as vulnerable. This strategy may not seem the stuff of high policy, but its potential is great, given time. The power of information technology is growing, and the power of truth should prevail in Serbia as it has elsewhere.

Of course, certainty of the success of long-term isolation is not essential to the case for maintaining it on the Serbs. Economic war in perpetuity against an unrepentant Serbia would send a strong signal that even when aggression is not stopped it will result in unforgiving punishment. After all, if international law supports punitive action against aggressors who fail, is it not more important to punish those who succeed? In any case, if sanctions do not produce sweeping change in Belgrade, a crippled Serbia is preferable to one that is given the chance to rebound from its offensive war.

In the course of an international cold war against Serbia, at least scattered fighting would persist in Bosnia. The West cannot prevent this. It is mainly a consequence of the presence of a half-dozen Muslim enclaves in regions of Bosnia otherwise controlled by the Serbs. The Serbs may or may not try to force or pressure the Muslims to leave the enclaves. Now that the threat of NATO air strikes is present, the Serbs will likely be content to tolerate most if not all of these pockets. Muslims may attempt limited counteroffensives now and then. But, on balance, there is little reason to think the fighting will increase or spread, or that the main battle lines will shift.[2] Indeed, there may be a chance now of achieving a general or at least widespread ceasefire, decoupled from a definitive political solution. This war is terrible, but not so terrible or unstable as to justify a bad final settlement now, when the Serbs have the upper hand.

The international community, meanwhile, should concentrate its military efforts on improving humanitarian deliveries. Convoys will get through if they have adequate ground and air escorts who are not only authorized but ordered to use all necessary force to discharge their duties. Those who interfere with U.N. relief efforts or harm U.N. personnel should be exposed to air attack and charged with war crimes. To the French and British, who say they might pull out of Bosnia if there is not a quick deal with the Serbs, the United States should offer air cover and make the case publicly that the right stance toward Serbia is steadiness not retreat.

---

[2] In the unlikely event that the U.N. Security Council lifts the arms embargo on the Muslims, violence would increase, relief operations would be curtailed, Western consciences would be cleared, but Serbian gains almost certainly would not be reversed.

If the situation can be stabilized and the fighting curtailed by local ceasefires and restrictions on military operations, so much the better. Make this, not a political settlement, the focus of negotiations. But the tragic error that followed the London conference must not be repeated: agreements and commitments must be enforced. The West cannot resolve this conflict on acceptable terms with limited air power. But it should leave no doubt that it will be used without hesitation to uphold U.N. decisions and to protect those who wear blue helmets. This threat can help stabilize Bosnia while Serbia is punished.

There never was an easy solution to the Yugoslav problem, and our failures so far have made the conflict even harder to settle on terms we will not come to regret. So horrible is the war that pressures to stop it now—by air strikes or concessions—are intense. Yet they are not intense enough to generate public and international support for the kind of decisive intervention that could produce a just settlement.

Although the West is not prepared to defeat Milošević militarily, it is not bound to cut a deal with him. Western impatience and guilt do not permit us to forgive the crime of forcing a million Muslims from their homes. We can reach a more acceptable outcome in time, with an acceptable Serbian leadership, by showing steadfastness we did in the larger Cold War. The United States can avoid sending American troops to police the result of the West's weak policies. Unless we hand him victory now, Milošević will lose a cold war, and real peace can then come to the Balkans.

America, A European Power

Richard Holbrooke

THE NEW SECURITY ARCHITECTURE

President Clinton made four trips to Europe last year. This commitment of presidential time and attention underlines an inescapable but little-realized fact: the United States has become a European power in a sense that goes beyond traditional assertions of America's "commitment" to Europe. In the 21st century, Europe will still need the active American involvement that has been a necessary component of the continental balance for half a century. Conversely, an unstable Europe would still threaten essential national security interests of the United States. This is as true after as it was during the Cold War.

I do not intend, of course, to suggest that nothing has changed. The end of the Cold War, which can best be dated to that symbolic moment at midnight on December 25, 1991, when the Soviet flag came down over the Kremlin for the last time, began an era of change of historic proportions. Local conflicts, internal political and economic instability, and the return of historical grievances have now replaced Soviet expansionism as the greatest threat to peace in Europe. Western Europe and America must jointly ensure that tolerant democracies become rooted throughout all of Europe and that the seething, angry, unresolved legacies of the past are contained and solved.

Richard Holbrooke is Assistant Secretary of State for European and Canadian Affairs.

THE FOURTH ARCHITECTURAL MOMENT

ONLY THREE TIMES since the French Revolution has Europe peacefully reshaped its basic security architecture. Today, the continent is in the middle of nothing less than the fourth such moment in the last two centuries. The first post-Napoleonic security architecture for Europe, designed in 1815 at the Congress of Vienna, helped prevent all-out continental war for 99 years. The young United States, having fought two wars with England in only 40 years, successfully kept its distance, but for the last time.

In the second period of redesign, at Versailles in 1919, President Woodrow Wilson played a central role, but the United States withdrew almost immediately from the very structures it had helped create, thereby weakening them and thus virtually guaranteeing the tragic resumption of total war 20 years later. When the third opportunity arose in 1945, the great powers initially built a system based on Yalta, Potsdam, and the United Nations. But starting in 1947, when the leaders of the West realized that this system would not suffice to stem Soviet expansion, they created the most successful peacetime collective security system in history, centered around the Truman Doctrine, the Marshall Plan, NATO, Atlantic partnership—and American leadership.

This creative architecture reflected the underlying goals of America's postwar engagement in Europe. Its post-Cold War engagement must focus again on structures, old and new. This time, the United States must lead in the creation of a security architecture that includes and thereby stabilizes all of Europe—the West, the former Soviet satellites of central Europe, and, most critically, Russia and the former republics of the Soviet Union.

All the key participants in the new security equation in Europe—the United States, the West and central European countries, and the other nations of the former Soviet Union—desire a peaceful, stable, and democratic Russia, integrated into the institutions of an undivided Europe. No more important political goal has existed in Europe since a newly democratic West Germany was successfully integrated into the European political and security structure after World War II. It is for this and other reasons that the crisis in

Chechnya, discussed more fully below, has been so disturbing.

Fortunately, most of the great structures of the postwar period offer a usable foundation for building stability. The essential challenge is to maintain their coherence, project their influence, and adapt to new circumstances without diluting their basic functions.

Measured on the post-World War II calendar, the United States is now slightly past the point in the late spring of 1947 when Secretary of State George C. Marshall made his historic speech at Harvard University. The Marshall Plan he outlined that day was not charity. Rather, it was a program of assistance and credits designed to stimulate cooperation among the European states. And it is important to remember that Marshall offered the plan not only to Western Europe but to the Soviet Union, which turned it down for itself and its satellites and instead embarked on a 45-year epoch that condemned an entire region to political and economic ruin.

Those with the ability to preserve peace have the responsibility to build stable structures.

Today, as after World War II, early euphoria has yielded to a more sober appreciation of the problems, new and old. The tragedy of Bosnia does not diminish the responsibility to build a new comprehensive structure of relationships to form a new security architecture. On the contrary, Bosnia, the greatest collective security failure of the West since the 1930s, only underscores the urgency of that task.

In 1947, Americans learned that those with the ability to preserve the peace have a special responsibility to assist in building stable structures in newly democratic neighbors. Then only the United States was secure and prosperous enough to offer Western Europe the assistance it needed. Today an equally prosperous Western Europe (and Japan, which has a stake in and benefits from a stable Europe) will have to put up the bulk of the actual financial assistance, but the United States must continue to play a leading part. In the words of Secretary of State Warren Christopher, the central goal of the United States is "to help extend to all of Europe the benefits and obligations of the same liberal trading and collective security order that have been pillars of strength for the West."

A final lesson of the Marshall Plan is equally important. Those receiving support must build their own futures. The new democracies must contribute to their own security through both responsible behavior toward neighbors and democracy-building from within. The United States understands, welcomes, and encourages the desire of new European democracies to join the West through membership in its key institutions. But NATO, the European Union (EU), and the other major institutions of the West are not clubs that one joins simply by filling out membership applications. Over time, each has evolved values and obligations that must be accepted by each new member.

THE CHALLENGE OF CENTRAL EUROPE

ANY BLUEPRINT FOR the new security architecture of Europe must focus first on central Europe, the seedbed of more turmoil and tragedy in this century than any other area on the continent. The two most destructive wars in human history began from events on its plains, and the Cold War played itself out in its ancient and storied cities, all within the last 80 years.

Other historic watersheds also have not treated this area well. First the treaties of Versailles and Trianon, then the agreements of Yalta and Potsdam, and finally the collapse of the Soviet empire—those three benchmark events left throughout central Europe a legacy of unresolved and often conflicting historical resentments, ambitions, and, most dangerous, territorial and ethnic disputes. Without democracy, stability, and free-market economies, these lands remain vulnerable to the same problems, often exacerbated by an obsession with righting historical wrongs, real or mythical. If any of these malignancies spread—as they have already in parts of the Balkans and Transcaucasus—general European stability is again at risk. And for Germany and Russia, the two large nations on the flanks of central Europe, insecurity has historically been a major contributor to aggressive behavior.

But if there are great problems there are also great possibilities. For the first time in history, the nations of this region have the chance simultaneously to enjoy stability, freedom, and independence based on another first: the adoption of Western democratic ideals as a common foundation for all of Europe. The emotional but also practical lure of the West can be the strongest unifying force Europe has seen in generations, but only if unnecessary delay does not squander the opportunity.

The West owes much of its success to the great institutions created in the 1940s and 1950s. They serve an important internal function for their members, and they also project a sense of stability and security to others. If those institutions were to remain closed to new members, they would become progressively more isolated from new challenges and less relevant to the problems of the post-Cold War world. It would be a tragedy if, through delay or indecision, the West helped create conditions that brought about the very problems it fears the most. The West must expand to central Europe as fast as possible in fact as well as in spirit, and the United States is ready to lead the way. Stability in central Europe is essential to general European security, and it is still far from assured.

THE BUILDING BLOCKS

THE CENTRAL SECURITY pillar of the new architecture is a venerable organization: NATO. To some, the 45-year-old Atlantic alliance may seem irrelevant or poorly designed for the challenges of the new Europe. To others, NATO's extraordinary record of success may suggest that nothing needs to be changed. Both views are equally wrong. Expansion of NATO is a logical and essential consequence of the disappearance of the Iron Curtain and the need to widen European unity based on shared democratic values. But even before NATO expands, its strength and know-how are already playing an important role in building a new sense of security throughout Europe.

Designed decades ago to counter a single, clearly defined threat, NATO is only just beginning a historic transformation. NATO's core purpose of collective defense remains, but new goals and programs have been added. Collective crisis management, out-of-area force projection, and the encouragement of stability to the east through the Partnership for Peace (PFP) and other programs have been undertaken. Command structures have been streamlined. Static forces formerly concentrated to meet a possible Soviet attack across central Europe have been turned into more lightly armed, mobile, and flexible multinational corps designed to respond to a different, less stable world.

Two new structures—the North Atlantic Cooperation Council and the PFP—are specifically designed to reach out to countries that are not NATO members. They deserve closer attention, especially the creative new concept so appropriately named the Partnership for Peace. In just one year, this innovative idea has become an integral part of the European security scene, but it remains somewhat misunderstood and underestimated. Contrary to a fairly widespread impression, PFP is not a single organization; rather, it is a series of individual agreements between NATO and, at last count, 24 other countries ranging from Poland to Armenia, including Russia. Each "partner" country creates an individual program to meet its own needs.

Expansion of NATO is an essential consequence of the raising of the Iron Curtain.

PFP is an invaluable tool that encourages NATO and individual partners to work together. It helps newly democratic states restructure and establish democratic control of their military forces and learn new forms of military doctrine, environmental control, and disaster relief. In the future, it will provide a framework in which NATO and individual partners can cooperate in crisis management or out-of-area peacekeeping.

PFP proved its value immediately. In its first year of existence, allies and partners held joint military exercises in Poland, the Netherlands, and the north Atlantic. Ten partners have already established liaison offices with the NATO military command. Sixteen partners have begun joint activities with NATO, and others will follow. A defense planning and review process has been established within the partnership to advance compatibility and transparency between allies and partners. PFP is also a vehicle for partners to learn about NATO procedures and standards, thus helping each partner make an informed decision as to whether it wishes to be considered for membership in the alliance.

From the alliance perspective, PFP will provide a valuable framework for judging the ability of each partner to assume the obligations and commitments of NATO membership—a testing ground for their capabilities. And for those partners that do not become NATO members the PFP will provide a structure for increasingly close cooperation with NATO—in itself an important building block for European security. If U.S. hopes are realized, and the first year gives every reason to be optimistic, the PFP will be a permanent part of the European security scene even as NATO expands to take in some, but not all, PFP members.

EXPANDING NATO

NO ISSUE HAS been more important, controversial, or misunderstood than whether NATO should remain an alliance of its 16 current members or expand, and if it expands, why, where, when, and how. At the beginning of an important year on this issue, it is useful to clarify where the United States stands, and where it is going.

In essence, 1994 was the year in which, led by the United States, NATO decided it would eventually expand. This decision was reached during the January NATO summit in Brussels and reaffirmed by President Clinton during his return to Europe last June, when he stated that the question was no longer whether NATO would expand but how and when.

Last December, the NATO foreign ministers met again in Brussels, and, again led by the United States, they committed themselves to a two-phase program for 1995. During the first part of this year, NATO will determine through an internal discussion that is already under way the rationale and process for expanding the new, post-Cold War NATO. Then, in the months prior to the December 1995 ministerial meeting, NATO's views on these two issues—"why" and "how"—will be presented individually to PFP members who have expressed an interest in such discussions. This critical step will mark the first time detailed discussions on this subject have taken place outside the alliance. Then the ministers will meet again in Brussels in December and review the results of the discussions with the partners before deciding how to proceed.

This process, which at every stage requires the agreement of all 16 NATO members, is still in its initial stages. It is not yet widely understood. Given the importance of NATO, it is not surprising that some outside observers wish to accelerate the process while others do not want it to commence at all. The Clinton administration and its NATO allies, after some initial disagreements, have chosen a gradual and deliberate middle course—and have begun the process.

Several key points should be stressed:

• First, the goal remains the defense of the alliance's vital interests and the promotion of European stability. NATO expansion must strengthen security in the entire region, including nations that are not members. The goal is to promote security in central Europe by integrating countries that qualify into the stabilizing framework of NATO.

• Second, the rationale and process for NATO's expansion, once decided, will be transparent, not secret. Both Warsaw and Moscow, for example, will have the opportunity to hear exactly the same presentation from NATO later this year, and both should have access to all aspects of the alliance's thinking in order to understand that NATO should no longer be considered an anti-Russian alliance. As former National Security Adviser Zbigniew Brzezinski, an advocate of rapid expansion, wrote in the January/February 1995 issue of *Foreign Affairs*, "Neither the alliance nor its prospective new members are facing any imminent threat. Talk of a 'new Yalta' or of a Russian military threat is not justified, either by actual circumstances or even by worst-case scenarios for the near future. The expansion of NATO should, therefore, not be driven by whipping up anti-Russian hysteria that could eventually become a self-fulfilling prophecy."

• Third, there is no timetable or list of nations that will be invited to join NATO. The answers to the critical questions of who and when will emerge after completion of this phase of the process.

• Fourth, each nation will be considered individually, not as part of some grouping.

• Fifth, the decisions as to who joins NATO and when will be made exclusively by the alliance. No outside nation will exercise a veto.

• Sixth, although criteria for membership have not been determined, certain fundamental precepts reflected in the original Washington treaty remain as valid as they were in 1949: new members must be democratic, have market economies, be committed to responsible security policies, and be able to contribute to the alliance. As President Clinton has stated, "Countries with repressive political systems, countries with designs on their neighbors, countries with militaries unchecked by civilian control or with closed economic systems need not apply."

• Lastly, it should be remembered that each new NATO member constitutes for the United States the most solemn of all commitments: a bilateral defense treaty that extends the U.S. security umbrella to a new nation. This requires ratification by two-thirds of the U.S. Senate, a point that advocates of immediate expansion often overlook.

A BROAD CONCEPT OF SECURITY

NATO EXPANSION CANNOT occur in a vacuum. If it did, it would encourage the very imbalances and instabilities it was seeking to avoid. In addition to NATO, a variety of organizations and institutions must contribute to the new structure of peace. The new architecture should involve both such institutions as NATO and the EU, which strive for true integration among members, and others such as the Organization for Security and Cooperation in Europe (OSCE), which provide a wide, inclusive framework for looser forms of cooperation.

Although the EU is primarily a political and economic entity, it also makes an important contribution to European security. The integration of West European nations has virtually transcended the territorial disputes, irredentist claims, social cleavages, and ethnic grievances that tore apart European societies in earlier eras.

The extension of the EU eastward (and southward, if Cyprus and Malta join) will therefore be immensely important. It will integrate and stabilize the two halves of Europe. This process began with the entry of Austria, Finland, and Sweden at the beginning of this year. Europe agreements committed the EU and six central European nations to industrial free trade on January 1, 1995, except in steel and textiles, which will follow in 1996 and 1998. Slovenia and the Baltic states are expected to sign similar agreements soon. In December, the EU heads of state and government agreed on a "pre-accession" strategy for eventual entry, presumably sometime early in the next century, of the central European states, Cyprus, and Malta. For Germany, which, in Chancellor Helmut Kohl's powerful phrase, "cannot remain indefinitely Europe's eastern boundary," the extension of the EU is especially important, which is why Germany led this move during its term in the EU presidency.

Expansion of NATO and the EU will not proceed at exactly the same pace. Their memberships will never be identical. But the two organizations are clearly mutually supportive. Although the relationship between NATO and the EU is complex, particularly as the EU seeks to define its relationship with the WEU to create a European defense identity, it is clearly mutually supportive; the expansion of both are equally necessary for an undivided and stable Europe.

It would be self-defeating for the WEU to create military structures to duplicate the successful European integration already achieved in NATO. But a stronger European pillar of the alliance can be an important contribution to European stability and transatlantic burden-sharing, provided it does not dilute NATO. The WEU establishes a new premise of collective defense: the United States should not be the only NATO member that can protect vital common interests outside Europe.

STRENGTHENING THE OSCE

NEITHER NATO NOR the EU can be everything to everyone, and the other organizations above are focused on narrower issues. There is, therefore, a need in the new European architectural concept for a larger, looser region-wide security organization—smaller, of course, than the United Nations—that offers a framework for dealing with a variety of challenges that neither NATO nor the EU is designed to address, one that includes both NATO members and other countries on an equal basis.

Fortunately, the core for such a structure has existed for some years—the Conference on Security and Cooperation in Europe. Its 53-nation structure of human rights commitments, consultations, and efforts at cooperative or preventive diplomacy was intended to fill a niche in the new Europe. Born out of the 1975 Helsinki Accords, the CSCE unexpectedly provided, through its famous Basket III, a lever on human rights and democratic values that played a major role in undermining communism. But it was clear by the middle of last year that the CSCE, while offering intriguing possibilities, had neither the internal coherence nor the political mandate to meet the challenges facing it.

Moscow and the major NATO allies shared this view. By the fall of last year, all had agreed that as NATO began to look at expansion, the CSCE should be strengthened and upgraded. A significant evolution of this organization, including a name change, began in December 1994 at the Budapest summit attended by President Clinton and Secretary Christopher. The result was a series of steps toward a clearer political and operational mandate, a strengthened consultative apparatus, and a new status. The old "conference" became a full-fledged "organization," and the OSCE was born.

The role of the new OSCE must now be more clearly established. Rather than enforcing behavior through legal or military action, it seeks to improve security by building new forms of cooperation based on consensus. With a membership that literally spans all 24 time zones and a huge array of cultures and nations, OSCE members will often disagree on how its standards are to be implemented. Taking such disagreement as a given, the OSCE must be more aggressive in the search for common ground.

Today security in Europe requires addressing potential conflicts earlier. The OSCE must prove its worth in this area, as the CSCE did in spreading democratic values and legitimizing human rights. The organization has pioneered efforts, however limited, at conflict prevention and crisis management through innovations such as establishing a high commissioner for national minorities and sending resident missions to conflict areas. More must be done.

The United States has taken the lead in pursuing innovations within the OSCE. In the future, the United States will make more vigorous use of the OSCE's consultative and conflict prevention mechanisms. The goal is to establish the OSCE as an integral element of the new security architecture. In a time of great burdens for the United Nations, the OSCE, as a regional organization under Chapter VII of the U.N. Charter, can perform many functions normally expected from the United Nations. The participation of U.N. Secretary General Boutros Boutros-Ghali in the OSCE Budapest summit underlined the importance of such cooperation.

Under no circumstances can the OSCE be a substitute for NATO or the EU. The OSCE can in no way be superior to NATO; the functions of the two organizations are and shall remain entirely different. Conversely, expansion of the role of the OSCE does not conflict with the responsibilities of NATO. Its methods occupy a totally different dimension than those of NATO.

A recent example of this function was the agreement reached at Budapest between Russia and the OSCE to merge negotiating efforts on the difficult issue of Nagorno-Karabakh and provide peacekeeping troops once a political agreement is reached—important steps on the OSCE's path to becoming a more meaningful organization. More recently, the Russians agreed to an OSCE fact-finding mission on Chechnya. The very fact that Moscow accepted OSCE involvement is significant, but this involvement came far too late and is too limited.

> In Chechnya, Russia should adhere to international standards of human rights.

Without question Chechnya is part of the Russian Federation. At the same time, the United States has maintained from the outset that the Russian government should adhere to international standards, enshrined in OSCE resolutions and elsewhere, of respect for human rights. Tragically and unnecessarily, the Russian government prosecuted its military campaign against the city of Grozny in ways certain to cause large numbers of civilian casualties and hinder humanitarian assistance.

The West's overall objective in Russia and the rest of the former Soviet Union remains integration—bringing emerging democracies into the fold of Western political, economic, and security institutions. From the beginning of the battle for Grozny, Chechnya worked in exactly the opposite direction for Russia. Chechnya also has proved a deeply divisive element in Russian political life and has become a serious setback for the cause of reform, democratization, and the evolution of the Russian Federation as a stable, democratic, multiethnic state. The Chechnya conflict, terrible though it is, has not changed the nature of U.S. interests. President Clinton stated in January that, as Russia undergoes a historic transformation, reacting reflexively to each of the ups and downs that it is bound to experience, perhaps for decades to come, would be a terrible mistake. If the forces of reform are embattled, the United States must reinforce, not retreat from, its support for them.

The U.S. objective remains a healthy Russia—a democratic Russia pursuing reform and respecting the rights of its citizens, not fragmenting into ethnic conflict and civil war. America's ability to pursue and develop its partnership with Russia depends on a common pursuit of these values and objectives. The reason Russia has qualified as a friend and partner of the United States is that its people and government have embarked on a path of democratization, development of an open civil society, and respect for basic human rights. That is what the United States continues to support in Russia.

RUSSIA AND UKRAINE

To REPEAT: if the West is to create an enduring and stable security framework for Europe, it must solve the most enduring strategic problem of Europe and integrate the nations of the former Soviet Union, especially Russia, into a stable European security system. Russia is already involved in most aspects of the emerging architecture. It participates actively in the OSCE and worked closely with the United States in upgrading that organization. Russia has signed an ambitious partnership agreement with the EU. It has joined the Partnership for Peace with NATO. It is a candidate for membership in the Council of Europe. The United States supports deeper Russian participation in the Group of Seven industrialized nations and is sponsoring Russia's membership in the World Trade Organization, successor to the General Agreement on Tariffs and Trade. For the first time since 1945, Russia is participating, as a member of the Contact Group on Bosnia, in a multinational negotiating team presenting a unified position on a difficult security issue.

Enhancement of stability in central Europe is a mutual interest of Russia and the United States. NATO, which poses no threat to Russian security, seeks a direct and open relationship with Russia that both recognizes Russia's special position and stature and reinforces the integrity of the other newly independent states of the former Soviet Union. There have been proposals, including one by Russian President Boris Yeltsin in late 1993, for a special arrangement between NATO and Russia, which could take a number of forms. In urging rapid expansion of NATO, Brzezinski proposed in his *Foreign Affairs* article a "formal treaty of global security cooperation between NATO and the Russian Federation," in conjunction with an upgrade of the OSCE.

Any negotiations between NATO and Russia on this or any other arrangement would be quite complex. They would need to take into account a wide range of factors, including the pace of NATO expansion, the state of other Russian-NATO ties such as the Partnership for Peace, the degree to which the OSCE has been turned into a more useful organization, and the implications of events such as the fighting in Chechnya. Notwithstanding this array of issues, the U.S. government as well as its major allies have supported development of this important new track in the European security framework. Informal discussions of this possibility, while in a highly preliminary phase, began in January when Secretary Christopher met in Geneva with Russian Foreign Minister Andrei Kozyrev.

Any such arrangement must consider the special case of Ukraine. Its geostrategic position makes its independence and integrity a critical element of European security. In Budapest last December, President Clinton and the leaders of Belarus, Kazakhstan, Russia, and Ukraine exchanged documents of ratification for the Strategic Arms Reduction Treaty, formally bringing START I into force. At the same time, Ukraine also deposited its instrument of accession to the Nuclear Nonproliferation Treaty, and the United States, Russia, and the United Kingdom provided security assurances to Belarus, Kazakhstan, and Ukraine.

The basic goals of those seeking to take advantage of this moment in history are the expansion of democracy and prosperity, the integration of political and security institutions, and a unity that has always eluded Europe, even with American involvement. Leaders will have to lead to break through the layers of ambivalence, confusion, complacence, and history that inhibit reforms. As the great architect of European unity, Jean Monnet, observed, "Nothing is possible without men, but nothing is lasting without institutions." The efforts of Monnet, Marshall, and others produced unparalleled peace and prosperity for half a century—but for only half a continent. The task ahead is as daunting as its necessity is evident. To turn away from the challenge would only mean paying a higher price later.

Making Peace with the Guilty

The Truth about Bosnia

Charles G. Boyd

> English persons, therefore, of humanitarian and reformist disposition constantly went out to the Balkan Peninsula to see who was in fact ill-treating whom, and, being by the very nature of their perfectionist faith unable to accept the horrid hypothesis that everybody was ill-treating everybody else, all came back with a pet Balkan people established in their hearts as suffering and innocent, eternally the massacree and never the massacrer.
>
> Rebecca West
> *Black Lamb and Grey Falcon*, 1938

REBECCA WEST loved the peoples of the Balkans, but she is not the only traveler to return from there with some measure of cynicism. For more than two years, I have found myself increasingly consumed and frustrated by events in the former Yugoslavia. I have traveled to the region on several occasions and have had the advantage of hearing the personal views of young men and women in Croatia and Macedonia assigned to the American forces, the U.N. Protection Force (UNPROFOR), and the U.N. High Commissioner for Refugees.

The views I share here are the product of seeing this war up close,

---

GENERAL CHARLES G. BOYD, USAF (RET.), was the Deputy Commander in Chief, U.S. European Command, from November 1992 to July 1995. A fighter pilot and combat veteran of Vietnam, he held many senior command and staff positions throughout his 35-year military career.

almost continuously, in all its ugliness. These views differ from much of the conventional wisdom in Washington, which is stunted by a limited understanding of current events as well as a tragic ignorance or disregard of history. Most damaging of all, U.S. actions in the Balkans have been at sharp variance with stated U.S. policy.

The linchpin of the U.S. approach has been the underinformed notion that this is a war of good versus evil, of aggressor against aggrieved. From that premise the United States has supported U.N. and NATO resolutions couched in seemingly neutral terms—for example, to protect peacekeepers—and then has turned them around to punish one side and attempt to affect the course of the war. It has supported the creation of safe areas and demanded their protection even when they have been used by one warring faction to mount attacks against another. It has called for a negotiated resolution of the conflict even as it has labeled as war criminals those with whom it would negotiate. It has pushed for more humanitarian aid even as it became clear that this was subsidizing conflict and protecting the warring factions from the natural consequences of continuing the fighting. It has supported the legitimacy of a leadership that has become increasingly ethnocentric in its makeup, single-party in its rule, and manipulative in its diplomacy.

All factions are pursuing the same objective: not to be a minority.

To take one example: recently more than 90 percent of the Serbs in western Slavonia were ethnically cleansed when Croatian troops overran that U.N.-protected area in May. As of this writing this Croatian operation appears to differ from Serbian actions around the U.N. safe areas of Srebrenica and Zepa only in the degree of Western hand-wringing and CNN footage the latter have elicited. Ethnic cleansing evokes condemnation only when it is committed by Serbs, not against them.

We must see things in the Balkans as they are, not as we wish them to be. We must separate reality from image. Is it possible that all sides have legitimate interests and fears, or does legitimacy remain the special province of only one or two factions? We need a healthy skepticism about accepted "wisdom," and above all, we need to tell the truth, if only to ourselves.

THE OBJECTIVES

ALL FACTIONS in the former Yugoslavia have pursued the same objective—avoiding minority status in Yugoslavia or any successor state—and all have used the tools most readily available to achieve that end. For the Croats that meant a declaration of independence from a Yugoslav federation increasingly dominated by Serb nationalism and an appeal to the European Union for recognition. The new state identified itself and full citizenship within it as Croatian and claimed sovereignty extending to the boundaries of the old Croat Republic of the Yugoslav federation. Bosnia's Muslims had no such option as they were a plurality, not a majority, on their territory. They were also considerably less enthusiastic about leaving the federation, recognizing that with its explosive population mix, Bosnia seemed to make more sense as part of a larger multiethnic Yugoslavia than as a stand-alone entity. The secession of Slovenia and Croatia left a rump Yugoslavia formed around Serbia and Montenegro an even less hospitable home, however, and Bosnia's Muslims too opted for secession.

In recognizing the new Bosnian state, the international community demanded, and Bosnia's Muslims (and some of their Serb and Croat neighbors) delivered, a commitment to democracy and individual rights that made the nations of the West comfortable with their own commitment to the new Bosnian state. Their approach was tactically sound and, as a practical matter, the only course available to Bosnia's well-educated but under-armed Muslim plurality if it was to preserve its newly proclaimed independence. Pointing this out does not diminish the essential nobility of this course, nor the obvious moral advantage it gave the new state in comparison with some of its neighbors.[1]

In this atmosphere of fear, uncertainty, and resurgent nationalism, first the Croatian and then the Bosnian Serbs—with Serbian sup-

[1] Regrettably, the Bosnian polity had organized itself into political parties based largely on ethnic identity. As the world moved toward recognition of the Bosnian state, Bosnian President Alija Izetbegović's Party of Democratic Action and its Croat and Serb counterparts exercised near-absolute control over regions where their ethnic groups were in the majority. Izetbegović's party today runs Bosnia as a one-party state.

port—took up arms to do what international recognition had done for the Croats of Croatia and the Muslims of Bosnia: ensure that they would not be a minority in a state they perceived to be hostile. What is frequently referred to as rampant Serb nationalism and the creation of a greater Serbia has often been the same volatile mixture of fear, opportunism, and historical myopia that seems to motivate patriots everywhere in the Balkans. Much of what Zagreb calls the occupied territories is in fact land held by Serbs for more than three centuries, ever since imperial Austria moved Serbs to the frontier (the Krajina) to protect the shopkeepers of Vienna (and Zagreb) from the Ottomans. The same is true of most Serb land in Bosnia, what the Western media frequently refers to as the 70 percent of Bosnia seized by rebel Serbs. There were only 500,000 fewer Serbs than Muslims in Bosnia at independence, with the more rural Serbs tending toward larger landholdings. In short, the Serbs are not trying to conquer new territory, but merely to hold on to what was already theirs.

The Serbs are not trying to conquer new territory but to hold on to what was already theirs.

These are not minor historical points. The twin poles of much of Western diplomacy in the Balkans and elsewhere have been self-determination and the inviolability of borders. In the cases of Croatia and Bosnia, as well as Slovenia and Macedonia, Western nations suffered a temporary lapse in their concern over borders, accepting the dissolution of a U.N. member nation in favor of self-determination. That policy contributed to stability where the will of the population was most clear—ethnically homogeneous Slovenia—and led to catastrophic destabilization where the will of the population was most ambiguous—ethnically mixed Bosnia. One-third of Bosnia's population boycotted the referendum on independence and made it unmistakably clear that it would take up arms if the new state was created and recognized.

There are legitimate concerns over what constitutes an appropriate unit of self-determination; the United States cannot possibly support ever-shrinking pockets of ethnic preference. But the United States hobbles its understanding of this conflict if it imputes its global concerns to the local players. As one Serb officer confided to a member of my staff, he did not understand why his people had been "satanized" for insisting on the same right of self-determination that had been accorded virtually all others in the former Yugoslavia.

War in Bosnia and Croatia was not the inevitable product of centuries of ethnic hatreds. It was created from ambition, fear, and incompetence—local and international.

THE CONDUCT OF THE WAR

NO ONE of conscience can ignore the moral dimension of this crisis. Unspeakable acts have been perpetrated on the innocent. I have flown over Bosnian villages and seen the results, not of combat, but of ethnically based criminal violence, homes within a village selectively and systematically destroyed as the majority population—Muslim, Serb, or Croat—cleansed its community of now unwanted minorities. I have walked the streets of villages like Gornji Vakuf and seen the faces of angry, armed young men staring at one another across city squares and streets transformed into ethnic confrontation lines. No one can visit Mostar and witness the city's historic center—made rubble by small arms fire—and not feel and fear how thin the veneer of civility must be for us all. And as one turns every corner in Sarajevo to be greeted by more destruction, it is difficult to escape the questions, what manner of man is in those hills, and what possessed him to pull the lanyard on his artillery?

But to make rational judgments of policy requires a depth of understanding that goes beyond a transient image or sound bite. For some, the war in Bosnia has become a tragedy of proportions that parallel the Holocaust, an example of plain good against stark evil. For these people, the Serbs are the forces of darkness, responsible for most if not all of the atrocities, the ethnic cleansing, mass rapes, concentration camps, and indiscriminate killing.

Regrettably, that behavior is not unprecedented in Balkan conflicts, and to say that it is peculiarly Serb behavior says more about the observer than the Balkans. If one comes into the movie in 1991 or 1992, a case can be made that the Serbs indeed are the villains of this picture, but to ignore the previous reels will, at a minimum, impair divining the ultimate plot line. And let me dare to suggest that my observations tell me that even today's picture is more complex than is generally regarded. The public view of this war has come largely through the eyes of one party, a people, as Rebecca West warned, whose status as victim has been a valuable and jealously protected tool of war. Make no mistake: Serb behavior has been reprehensible. The question is how bad? On what scale? And how unique? Analysis of what has happened is not a claim of moral equivalence, nor is it a justification for the actions being examined.

How bad has this war been? When one drives past the destroyed speed-skating rink and the Olympic stadium in Sarajevo, the eye involuntarily turns to row upon row of markers atop fresh graves dug in the new and largest cemetery in the capital. Clearly, thousands have died in Sarajevo. How many people have died in this war overall? Nobody knows. The Bosnian government has an interest in portraying the number as high as possible: it is a testament to the savagery of their opponent, a cry for assistance and at the same time an indictment of a cautious international community. Until recently the government claimed the number of dead and missing to be about 250,000. Many have been skeptical of that figure, with some suggesting the real number could be as low as 25,000, although other estimates—including my own—are more frequently in the 70,000 to 100,000 range. In April the government lowered its estimate to just over 145,000, about 3 percent of the prewar population. That is a sobering number, but even accepting it at face value and granting that it is unevenly distributed across the population, does that total after 38 months of warfare make charges of genocide a meaningful contribution to policy debate?

Sarajevo is instructive. The government estimate puts the death toll in the capital just above 10,000. Someone has calculated that the city has been hit by 600,000 shells, and some 60 percent of its buildings have been destroyed or severely damaged. Recent fighting, shelling, and harassment of humanitarian convoys have once again increased the city's suffering and isolation. What normalcy that exists there is a tribute to international relief efforts and, above all, the courage and resilience of the city's population.

The city's actual suffering, however, does not change the reality that the image of Sarajevo, battered and besieged, is a valuable tool for the Bosnian government. As that government was commemorating the thousandth day of the siege, local markets were selling oranges, lemons, and bananas at prices only slightly higher than prices in western Europe. At the same time the commercial price of gasoline in Sarajevo was 35 percent cheaper than gasoline in Germany. A World Food Programme survey in May 1994 found that, after a tough winter for Sarajevo, no one in the city was malnourished, and only a small percentage of the population was undernourished. Even the rate of violent deaths had gone down considerably in 1994 (324 for the year according to the United Nations; the per capita rate was comparable to some North American cities and slightly lower than Washington, D.C.), although press coverage and government statements gave the image of unrelenting siege.

Some of the city's suffering has actually been imposed on it by actions of the Sarajevo government. Some were understandable policies, like the restriction on travel to prevent the depopulation of the city during those periods when movement was possible. Others were the by-product of government weakness, like relying on the Sarajevo underworld for the initial defense of the city, thereby empowering criminal elements that took their toll on the population, especially Serbs. Still others were intentional; whether out of individual greed or official policy is unclear. Government soldiers, for example, have shelled the Sarajevo airport, the city's primary lifeline for relief supplies. The press and some governments, including that of the United States, usually attribute all such fire to the Serbs, but no seasoned observer in Sarajevo doubts for a moment that Muslim forces have found it in their interest to shell friendly targets. In this case, the shelling usually closes the airport for a time, driving up the price of black-market goods that enter the city via routes controlled by Bosnian army commanders and government officials. Similarly, during the winter of 1993-94, the municipal government helped deny water to the city's population. An American foundation had implemented an innovative scheme to pump water into the city's empty lines, only to be denied permission by the government for health reasons. The denial had less to do with water purity than with the opposition of some Sarajevo officials who were reselling U.N. fuel donated to help distribute water. And, of course, the sight of Sarajevans lining up at water distribution points, sometimes under mortar and sniper fire, was a poignant image.

The war has also redrawn the demographic map of Bosnia; fear, combat, and nationalist extremism have displaced upwards of two million people. Much of this displacement has been forced population movements, the engine for much of which has been Serbian—Serb fear, Serb security demands, and Serb cruelty. When the Serbs took up arms in the spring of 1992, their immediate aim was to secure their communities from real and imagined threats from their non-Serb neighbors. With this accomplished, they moved to connect Serb areas with secure lines of communication through locations in which other ethnic groups were dominant. In both operations, non-Serbs were viewed as security threats and cleansed from the territory in question. In a campaign that appeared to reflect central direction and planning, Serb excesses were common and well documented.

Less generally known are Serb population movements. During a visit to Sarajevo in February a senior U.N. official told me that there may be as few as 500,000 Serbs on Serb-held territory in Bosnia. Combined with the 200,000 Serbs that he estimated are living on Bosnian-controlled land, the Serb population in Bosnia may be only about half its prewar total. Like their former neighbors, Bosnia's Serbs can point to fear, combat, and forced expulsion as the reasons for their movement, although the proportions are likely different.

Serbian people have suffered when hostile forces have advanced, with little interest or condemnation by Washington or CNN correspondent Christiane Amanpour. Late in 1994, when the Bosnian V Corps broke out of the Bihać pocket, they burned villages as they went and forced several thousand Serbs to flee. The same happened when Bosnian Croat forces pushed up the Livno valley shortly thereafter. If anyone doubts the capacity of Bosnia's non-Serb population to inflict ethnic cruelty, let him or her visit the Croat enclaves around Kiseljak or Vitez. The scarred shells of Catholic churches and Muslim mosques as well as thousands of private homes give ample testimony to the barbarity of Muslim and Croat violence, and these Muslim and Croat troops likely did what they did for much the same reasons as their Serb neighbors: revenge for real and alleged sins of the past and the perceived demands of present security. There are times when the distinctions among the factions appear more a question of power and opportunity than morality.

THE FUTURE COURSE OF THE WAR

THE STRATEGIC situation on the ground has changed substantially since the war began. Three years of fear, combat, and crime masquerading as battle have effected great change. With their enclaves largely preserved, Croats see their future more in their relationship with Zagreb than with Sarajevo. And with the 1993-94 combat and atrocities a fresh memory, they view their Muslim federation partners with distrust, frequently echoing Serb fears of the encroachment of Islam into Christian Europe. Bosnia's Croats joined the federation to get out of the Bosnian war (which they were losing) and have little interest in joining any sustained campaigns against Bosnia's Serbs. This is not true of Bosnia's Muslims and Serbs. Without question, these factions each intend to win this war. The Serbs think they have won already and want the war to end. The Muslims know they have not and are seeking ways to continue it.

Serbs suffer from the general depopulation of the areas they control; economic activity is depressed, and they are hard-pressed to marshal forces. The popular image of this war is one of unrelenting Serb expansion, but much of Bosnia has historically been Serb, and the recent Serb moves against the eastern enclaves represent the only significant changes in their area of control in nearly two years.

Muslims have been largely forced into the central core of the country. This has provided the Sarajevo government with a strong base and internal lines of communication with which to take the fight to extended Serb units. The refugee population that forms the core of the Bosnian army guarantees a numerical advantage (150,000-200,000 to 80,000) and ensures a continued will to fight to recapture lost territory.

Even the Serb advantage in heavy equipment is not what it once was. The closure of the Serbian border by Belgrade is incomplete and imperfect but nonetheless real. It has affected Bosnian Serb access to fuel and equipment. Meanwhile, the flow of armaments passing to Bosnian forces continues almost unremarked upon by the international community. Senate Majority Leader Bob Dole's much-trumpeted desire to lift the embargo would be amusing but for the fact that it would almost certainly lead to the introduction of U.S. ground forces. The embargo has been lifted in all but name, to the delight of much of the U.S. policy elite. To be sure, since supplies must pass through Croatian territory, Zagreb controls the types of weapons that pass to Bosnia and continues to deny the heavy weapons that could challenge it in renewed Muslim-Croat fighting. Nonetheless, the Muslims' forces are vastly better off than they were earlier in the war. The armies in Bosnia—Serb and Muslim—are asymmetrical in their military power, but they are very closely matched. Serbian successes against the eastern enclaves in July were small-scale operations against isolated, demoralized units. That Serbian units did not attack the government army in central Bosnia—Sarajevo's real center of gravity—is a reflection of this new balance. And time is quite likely on the side of the Muslims.

The distinction among the factions is more power and opportunity than morality.

It is a remarkable achievement of Bosnian diplomacy, and one reinforced by the government's rhetoric after the fall of Srebrenica, that the Muslims have been able to gain significant military parity with the Serbs, while nonetheless maintaining the image of hapless victim in the eyes of much of the world community. It is all the more remarkable since, before the Srebrenica attack, the Muslims had been on the strategic offensive for more than a year.

In this campaign the Muslims have consistently tried to use the United Nations and NATO (with the attendant safe areas, no-fly zones, exclusion zones, and demilitarized zones) as a shield, allowing themselves to weaken their forces in one area—depending on the United Nations or the international community to protect it—while concentrating their forces elsewhere. In the winter of 1993-94 the Sarajevo government stripped the capital's defenses to release troops to fight against the Croats in central Bosnia, counting on their public diplomacy efforts to manage the risk to Sarajevo. It was a near-run thing, but in the end the city was protected by the threat of NATO air strikes and the imposition of a heavy-weapons exclusion zone.

This spring and summer the Muslims excoriated the United Nations for failing to protect Sarajevo, or as one U.N. official privately put it, for failing to do their fighting for them. Almost immediately after the Serb shelling of the tunnel under the Sarajevo airport—the only route open for Muslim military supplies and commercial goods—

the Bosnian government demanded NATO air strikes, attacked the passive attitude of UNPROFOR, and complained that the genocide was continuing; Sarajevo was still a death camp. Holocaust-like rhetoric was even more prominently featured in government statements following the mid-July fall of Srebrenica.

All of this is designed to enlist active military intervention in support of Muslim war aims. To date this campaign appears to have been successful in guaranteeing the Bosnian government against catastrophic failure in continuing to pursue the military option. The Bosnian army may suffer casualties and even significant defeats, but neither the existence of the Bosnian state nor its control over the core of its territory can be seriously jeopardized without provoking a sharp international response. Beyond this, the Sarajevo government hopes to prod NATO and particularly the United States into even more active intervention. French President Jacques Chirac's challenge to President Clinton to help the Bosnians defend Goražde and the latter's willingness to consider helicopter and air support for the operation suggest that the effort might yet bear fruit.

Last fall's action around Bihać—a portion of which is a U.N. safe area—is particularly instructive. The situation in this pocket is complex, even by Balkan standards. The Bosnian government unit there, the V Corps, was opposed by both Bosnian Serb forces and troops loyal to Fikret Abdić, usually described in Western press accounts as renegade Muslim units. Actually Abdić, a powerful local businessman, was a member of the Bosnian collective presidency (he outpolled Izetbegović in national elections) and had been expelled from the government (or broke with it, depending on your point of view) when Sarajevo rejected an internationally brokered peace agreement. Eager for profit and familiar with operating on the gray side of the law, Abdić established his own state and mutually profitable relationships with his Serb and Croat neighbors. These ties were one of the few examples of successful multiethnic cooperation in the Balkans.

The Bosnian V Corps was still a fighting force, however, and in a series of well-conducted campaigns it defeated Abdić's largely mercenary army. The V Corps then turned its attention to the Bosnian Serb forces that surrounded it, broke out of the pocket, and captured several hundred square kilometers of territory from a shaken Serb opponent.

Serb forces were hard-pressed, and to mount a counterattack they had to rely not only on forces in Bosnia but units in the Krajina of Croatia as well. Slowly the Serbs pushed the V Corps back to approximately the original lines of confrontation. The V Corps gave ground but was never defeated and remains an effective fighting force to this day. During the counterattack, however, the Bosnian government and many in the international community demanded that the United Nations and NATO protect the Bihać safe area from Serb aggression. A common theme was the impending humanitarian catastrophe if strong steps were not taken—even though this was a fight that the Muslim army had picked, there was limited damage to the safe area, and Bihać was the headquarters and garrison town of the Bosnian units that had mounted the attack. Finally, rather than work toward a cease-fire to fend off the looming tragedy, Bosnian government actions were clearly orchestrated to create the conditions for NATO air strikes, not a cessation of hostilities.

HOW TO MAKE PEACE

I BELIEVE that the U.S. approach to the war in Bosnia is torn by a fundamental contradiction. The United States says that its objective is to end the war through a negotiated settlement, but in reality what it wants is to influence the outcome in favor of the Muslims. The United States, for example, watched approvingly as Muslim offensives began this spring, even though these attacks destroyed a ceasefire Washington has supported. This duplicity, so crude and obvious to all in Europe, has weakened America's moral authority to provide any kind of effective diplomatic leadership. Worse, because of this, the impact of U.S. action has been to prolong the conflict while bringing it no closer to resolution.

The United States recognized the secession of Bosnia reluctantly, but having done that, it embraced the new state and both praised and supported its multiethnic character. Whether this character was ever real or had a reasonable chance of success is a fair subject of debate, but no reasonable person can believe that a unitary, multiethnic Bosnia is possible today. Nonetheless, Washington treats the Bosnian government as it—and perhaps the best of the Bosnian leadership—

hoped and dreamed the country would be. It is not. It is the representative of one warring faction.

More balanced American diplomats admit privately that the Bosnian Serbs—like their Muslim and Croat neighbors—are not without legitimate interests and concerns in this conflict. The United States rarely addresses the problem in this light and for much of the past three years has based its approach more on excluding than including the Serbs. Former President Jimmy Carter made this point following his December visit to Sarajevo and Pale when he commented to the author that negotiating with one side, condemning the other, and issuing ultimatums was unlikely to lead to any agreement.

The United States says it wants to stop the war but really wants to influence the outcome.

It is worse than that. Isolation and privation have helped legitimize in the eyes of Serbs the worst of the Serb nation, to make acceptable to the broader population the faction that said the world was their enemy, that they were history's victims and Europe's protectors, that so great was their danger that any measures were appropriate to their defense. Demonization has unleashed demons.

How then is the United States to make tomorrow better than today? The most imporant change is to start telling the truth. The result will be, aside from restoring some moral stature, to reduce the fighting.

To think with clarity about the former Yugoslavia that exists rather than the one the U.S. administration would prefer and then to speak with honesty about it will be very difficult given the distance this government has traveled down the road of Serb vilification and Muslim and Croat approval. But until the U.S. government can come to grips with the essential similarities between Serb, Croat, and Muslim and recognize that the fears and aspirations of all are equally important, no effective policy can possibly be crafted that would help produce an enduring peace. This truth, however difficult to acknowledge publicly at this late date, must at the very least be recognized privately so that a revamp of policy can proceed from clear and accurate premises.

The first step is for the United States to announce, and then follow through by its actions, that it really does oppose a military solution. That would require a cessation of all the nonsense rhetoric about lifting an embargo that has in reality long since been lifted and about leveling a playing field that is as nearly level as it is likely to get. As long as the free flow of arms through Croatia to Bosnia continues to be taxed by the Croats in terms of a percentage of the total plus a prohibition on most heavy weapons (which the Croats understandably do not want to face the next time they square off against the Muslims), the strategic balance that now exists in Bosnia will likely remain.

By turning a blind eye to these arms deliveries while screeching at Belgrade to stop whatever still continues across the Drina to the Bosnian Serbs, the United States does two things: one, it disqualifies itself as the fair and balanced intermediary in the peace process, and two, it sends a powerful signal to the Muslims that a military solution is acceptable and perhaps preferred, notwithstanding solemn public statements in support of the diplomatic process.

Once established as actually supporting the arms embargo, the United States can gain credibility by opposing military activity irrespective of the source. Strong public denunciation must follow all attacks by Bosnian Serbs, Bosnian government forces, or for that matter Croatian campaigns such as that against the Krajinian Serbs in the western sector. The quiet approval by the United States when the Muslim forces broke the Cessation of Hostilities Agreement must change to condemnation just as stern as that directed at the Bosnian Serbs as they captured Srebrenica. Moreover, an absolutely impartial use of NATO air power against any faction that violates a U.N. sanction, not just the Serbs, must also become the expected response that the United States supports if the antagonists are to be persuaded that violence is not acceptable. This, if nothing else, will certainly help reduce the dying.

The second step is to reinforce peace and cooperation where they are found. The Bosnian federation is a starting point. The slow progress of building Muslim-Croat cooperation highlights the difficulties ahead, but the major failing of the federation is not the pace of its progress but its biethnic nature. It includes none of the Serbs in Bosnia, many of whom live in government-controlled lands. If the United States is not anti-Serb—merely against criminals and those who would choose war over peace—it must address the status of these citizens. Making peace with the Serbs in federation territory and giving them an identity, political voice, and the potential for constitutional options comparable to

Bosnia's Croats would send a powerful signal to those in Bosnian Serb territory that there are options beyond war and isolation.

The third major step is to restart the negotiation process. In the Washington agreement that led to the federation, the United States treated Bosnia's Croats and Muslims as separate entities, accorded their leaders legitimacy, brokered a deal between the two that largely stopped the killing, sought the ratification of that deal from a foreign power (Croatia), and recognized the validity of constitutional ties from one of those ethnic communities to another state (again, Croatia). The Contact Group's approach to Bosnia's Serbs (largely driven by U.S. pressure) has been decidedly different—a take-it-or-leave-it map. Under these circumstances there are no incentives for the Bosnian government to negotiate or compromise. That leaves the Serbs with three choices: accept the Contact Group plan, respond to government military action, or drastically increase the level of violence to force a military decision. The current map is unacceptable, so the fighting continues.

A key to restarting the negotiation process may lie with the nation that has quietly, but continuously, been marginalized: Russia. The United States' apparent desire to minimize Russia's involvement in the peace process is difficult to comprehend but may be rooted in two fears: that Russia would balk at using the peace process to advance for the Muslims diplomatically what they could not achieve militarily; and that Russia, currently on the sidelines in the international community, would gain considerable prestige and renewed diplomatic status from a success in brokering a solution to the conflict.

Whether these fears existed or were justified in the past is no longer relevant. The United States has now reached the point where the Russians may be its best hope for facilitating a diplomatic solution. The United States, for reasons of credibility, cannot do so; it can talk effectively with only two sides and therefore is not in a position to lead the diplomatic effort. Likewise, the United States has coopted the other players of the Contact Group, except Russia. In this regard, the Russians are untainted and have more credibility with the Serbs. Perhaps only they can address the Serbs' deepest fears and give them the confidence no other party has been interested in providing. And the Russians may like this new role. It would give them foreign policy stature in the wake of their debacle in Chechnya and a chance to prove their willingness and ability to play a constructive diplomatic role. More important, it would give the West new hope for settling the conflict diplomatically where no other option seems viable. This significant role comes with a risk, but at this stage it is a worthwhile price the United States may have to pay to stop the war. If the marginalization of Russia has not alienated the latter beyond redemption, the United States should seek its full partnership immediately.

The hour is late in Bosnia. By the time you read this, the United States may not be able to prevent the withdrawal of U.N. forces; it may even be beyond its ability to resist the pressures to deploy American ground troops, goaded by a strangely bellicose press and anxious allies. But if the United States is to insert itself, it should do so without illusion. Without a determined policy choice to the contrary, it would in fact be entering not to reinforce the peace, but rather to help one faction win, a faction that has been maneuvering for such intervention since the Bosnian state was created. It would be allowing its European allies who, until now, have had the lead militarily in the Balkans, to transfer the tar now stuck to their fingers to the United States' and force America to assume the moral responsibility for the outcome of the conflict.

Only large numbers of troops on the ground can make a difference.

All this will be at considerable cost because in this conflict only very large numbers of troops on the ground will make a difference. Despite its appeal to the amateur strategist, a reliance on air power alone—the strike option—in this type of terrain with these kinds of targets has never held any real promise of conflict resolution. Given the political dynamics that developed after the fall of Srebrenica and Zepa and as Goražde seemed threatened, a strong response from NATO was necessary if further erosion of its credibility was to be avoided. And indeed, the use of "robust" air power can have an effect on Serb behavior, particularly if it is used without regard for civilian casualties. But it cannot make the Serbs want to live as an ethnic minority in a nation they perceive to be hostile. It can only reinforce the paranoia that drives them to continue the fight so relentlessly even now.

Pushing NATO to agree to the robust use of its air power, then, as with most of the other U.S. policy moves in the former Yugoslavia, is linked more to the immediacy of the evening newscasts than to a rational overall political objective. For that reason it can have no more than a near-term effect. At the end of the day the United States must face the reality that it cannot produce an *enduring* solution with military force—air or ground—only one that will last until it departs.

There is an alternative: proceed from the premise that all factions to the conflict have legitimate needs, not just Muslims and Croats. Leverage Belgrade and Zagreb equally to stop the flow of arms to Bosnia. Denounce the use of military force with equal indignation toward all perpetrators. Pressure the Bosnians to negotiate in good faith or risk true abandonment. Enlist the Russians both to represent and dampen Serb demands. Enforce a ceasefire impartially.

There need be no illusions about the future. Given the horrors of the last three years, rebuilding trust in Bosnia will take a very long time. True healing is beyond our means. The best we can hope for is to create the conditions for Bosnia to heal itself. The U.S. can aid in this process but only if it is willing to be honest, at least to itself.

Heading Off War in the Southern Balkans

Misha Glenny

BOSNIA AND MACEDONIA: TWINS

IN THE month prior to late June 1991, when war engulfed the former Yugoslavia, the presidents of two constituent republics, Alija Izetbegović of Bosnia and Kiro Gligorov of Macedonia, spared no effort trying to close the widening chasm between Serbia and Croatia. Both men understood that in the event of armed conflict their republics could be the bloodiest theaters of war. Bosnia was especially threatened because it formed a wedge between Serbs and Croats as they attempted to establish the borders of their new nation-states by force.

Macedonia, so far, has escaped the horrors that its twin, Bosnia, has suffered. Yet if war continues in the northern Balkans, a gradual destabilization of Macedonia is almost certain to magnify the threat to its existence and to the wider security of the southern Balkan region. Even with relative peace in the northern Balkans, the tensions between ethnic Albanians and Macedonians make for a fragile state.

The political problems facing Macedonia are remarkably similar to those that destroyed Bosnia. Throughout the Cold War, both republics depended on the Yugoslav federation to ward off the territorial claims of their more powerful neighbors. The majority populations of Bosnia and Macedonia are relative newcomers to the Balkan drama. The Muslim and Slavic Macedonians have assumed

---

MISHA GLENNY is the author of *The Fall of Yugoslavia: The Third Balkan War* and *The Rebirth of History: Eastern Europe in the Age of Democracy* and a former correspondent for the BBC World Service.

the character of a modern nation only since 1945, partly due to a gradual historical maturation and partly due to Marshal Josip Tito, the former Yugoslav dictator, who encouraged Macedonian development to dilute the influence of Serbs and Croats in Yugoslavia. Macedonians are no longer satisfied to be cast as extras, the role allotted them during World War II. This time they have claimed center stage by asserting the right to form the core of two new nation-states in the Balkans. This makes the current conflict more complicated than its predecessor of 1941-45.

But the chief similarity lies in the two nations' strategic importance for the region. Dominance of Bosnia is the key to control of the Adriatic coast. Macedonia is the only territory where the Balkan mountains can be traversed from north to south, from Belgrade to Thessaloníki, and west to east, from Durres to Istanbul. Consequently, these two territories have repeatedly suffered as the main theaters of war when European turmoil has thrown the constitutional order of the Balkan region into question. Their geostrategic importance is paramount.

In modern times, Bosnia and Macedonia have always required the protection of an external power to survive, be it the Austro-Hungarians, the Ottomans, or a federal Yugoslavia. Without such guarantees both republics have had to rely on the goodwill of their minority populations for stability and security: the Serbs and Croats in Bosnia, the Albanians in Macedonia. If that goodwill is withdrawn—as happened in Bosnia in 1992—the republic is finished.

Macedonia is now heading down the same path as Bosnia. Although ethnic Albanians do not have nearly the Serbs' and Croats' military power, Macedonia is even less well-equipped to defend itself than Bosnia was.

STUMBLING IN THE NORTH BALKANS

IGNORANCE OF this political reality has led to grave mistakes by international actors in the ongoing drama among Bosnians, Serbs, and Croats. A glaring example has been the Clinton administration's Bosnia policy, which has been ridiculed comprehensively by both opponents and supporters of the Bosnian government. The Bosnian government in Sarajevo feels betrayed because Washington's rhetoric in favor of a unified Bosnia was never backed by force. One should either wage war on behalf of the Bosnian government or clearly state that one has no intention of doing so. Washington's great mistake was that it did neither: it held out the prospect of intervention if the Bosnian government's position continued to deteriorate, then did nothing when it came to the crunch.

Clinton's pusillanimity, however, did not endear him to others. The Serbs perceive the Americans as chiefly responsible for the hardships created by U.N. sanctions (even though the sanctions were, of course, approved by all five permanent members of the Security Council). In addition, they believe that the demonization of the Serbs was designed in Germany and manufactured in the United States. The Russians have been alarmed by Clinton's apparent willingness to consider NATO air attacks without consulting them, in a region where Russia believes it has vital interests. The Europeans have been exasperated by Washington's vacillation, provoking one senior official involved in the mediation of the Yugoslav wars to tell the Americans "to piss or get off the pot." Indeed, U.S. presidential hopeful Senator Robert Dole's decision to introduce legislation calling for the lifting of the arms embargo on Bosnia was probably motivated more by the Senate majority leader's wish to embarrass the president at his weakest foreign policy point than by an overwhelming commitment to restoring peace in the northern Balkans.

Clinton held out the prospect of intervention to Bosnia, but did nothing in the crunch.

Some sympathy must be extended to the White House and State Department. In the 1992 presidential campaign, Clinton seized on the public disgust provoked by television coverage of the detention camps run by the Bosnian Serbs. Holding this banner of moral outrage aloft when he assumed office, he remained unaware that it was an insufficient weapon with which to attack the politically complex collapse of the Yugoslav federation. Moreover, the range and depth of foreign policy problems confronting the new Democratic admin-

istration were far greater than those facing President Bush, even in his last two years in office.

The core problem was the administration's inability to identify any U.S. interests in Croatia and Bosnia. Initially policy was guided purely by an emotional response to Serbian atrocities. However, the more deeply the United States became involved, the more this moral position was muddied by security implications. The conflict in the northern Balkans involves two key relationships—one with Russia, the other with Turkey—that America must redefine following the collapse of communism. In the case of Bosnia, Washington was unable to satisfy Turkish demands without alienating the Russians and vice versa, and this contributed to wild zigzags in policy.

The growing catalogue of failures, however, did not deter the United States from stepping up its interest and diplomatic activity in the area. Vice President Gore became the chief sponsor of the Washington accords, signed in March 1994, which envisaged a federation of Bosnia's Muslims and Croats and a confederation of this new Bosnian entity and Croatia. Following the Washington accords, the Croatian government agreed to lease part of the Adriatic island of Brač to the U.S. military, which established an intelligence-gathering center there.

The accords further increased the influence of Peter Galbraith, the U.S. ambassador to Zagreb, who became the key architect of a plan to reintegrate the rebel areas now controlled by separatist Croatian Serbs into Croatia proper. The plan would give the half million Croatian Serbs far more political autonomy than they held before the war in exchange for the reintegration of the territories they now hold—roughly 27 percent of the prewar nation. Throughout 1994, many commentators considered Galbraith's statements on domestic Croatian politics as authoritative as those of President Franjo Tudjman. Despite universal criticism, the White House clearly had no intention of running away from Balkan politics with its tail between its legs.

U.S. COMPETENCE IN THE SOUTH BALKANS

IF THE Bosnian and Croatian policies of the United States have been such a failure, how is it that the American approach to the delicate web restraining conflict in the southern Balkans has been so mature? It has been particularly impressive compared with the clownish efforts of the European Union (EU).

A breakdown in relations between Macedonia's Slav majority and Albanian minority would provoke an internal collapse. In such an event, three of Macedonia's neighbors (Albania, Serbia, and Bulgaria), if not more, would be forced to consider filling the resultant power vacuum. If war reaches Macedonia, it will no longer matter whether a solution to the Bosnian and Croatian wars can be found—a whole new series of conflicts, distinct from the northern Balkans except in their common origin, would begin.

Two axes are emerging, one dressed in the garb of Eastern Orthodoxy, one veiled in Islamic raiment. These axes run roughly along the geopolitical lines that divide Macedonia. Bulgaria plays a maverick role, entrenched in the Eastern Orthodox camp but historically at odds with both Greece and Serbia over a number of issues. Macedonia is isolated and caught between a unilateral commercial blockade by Greece, which has made fuel and raw materials scarce, and the U.N. sanctions against the rump Yugoslavia, which have deprived Macedonia of its major trading partner. Nevertheless, its very existence as a multinational state prevents the hardening of the two axes. If a war were fought over its territory, it is likely that the conflict would quickly assume some characteristics of an ethnic and religious war such as Bosnia's. This implies an ever-greater struggle for influence between the Belgrade/Athens axis and the Albanian/Turkish alliance.

The spillover of this struggle into the Aegean Sea would be most disturbing. Such a conflict would be much more disruptive to the immediate interests of the United States than the Bosnian war has been. In particular, it would threaten American lines of communication with the Middle East. The EU has never been as concerned as the United States with the strategic importance of the southern Balkans and the Aegean Sea. But the EU does have a special responsibility in the region because Greece is a member state.

> If Macedonia implodes, resolving war in Bosnia and Croatia will no longer matter much.

The disputes between Greece and three of its neighbors—Macedonia, Albania, and Turkey—highlight the extreme difficulties the EU faces in establishing a common foreign and security policy. Greece has used a variety of reasons to justify its persistent obstructionism. Athens has blocked an EU aid package to Albania (although it relented late last year), resisted Turkey's bid to enter a customs union with the EU (this too has been overcome), and imposed a blockade on Macedonia. Greece has asserted that use of the name "Macedonia" by the former Yugoslav republic implied a claim on the neighboring Greek province of Macedonia. It also objected to Macedonia's use of a Hellenic symbol, the Star of Vergina, which consists of 16 rays surrounding a sunlike disk. It was the emblem of Alexander the Great's dynasty in the fourth century B.C.; Alexander was an ancient Makedon (who bear no relation to the Slav Macedonians of today) whose dominion included Greece. Western diplomats and U.N. officials stationed in Macedonia argue that the blockade worsens the economic difficulties the landlocked state faces. This in turn, they say, undermines relations between Albania and Macedonia, the cornerstone of the latter's stability.

Legally challenged by the EU, Athens justified its actions by claiming that Macedonia was a national security threat. This was a ludicrous argument, but legally the only one that Greece could use to override Maastricht treaty trade statutes. The remaining 11 EU members oppose Greece's regional policy, but they can do nothing about it, and the blockade remains in effect. Public admonishments and mediation efforts have only raised anti-EU sentiment in Greece.

While Greece's stance on Macedonia is self-defeating and presented in an infuriatingly emotional manner, the EU's inability to conduct subtle and effective diplomacy in a region where major armed conflict remains a distinct possibility is disturbing. The contrast is stark between the chaotic, failed diplomacy of the EU and the subtle, if sometimes opaque, American strategy. U.S. policy in the southern Balkans generally suffers from agency overkill. The White House, the State and Defense Departments, and the local embassies are all running apparently separate programs that seem to be heading generally in the same direction but often along different paths. In addition, there have been sharp differences of interpretation among the U.S. diplomatic missions in Belgrade, Zagreb, Sarajevo, Skopje, Sofia, Tirana, Athens, and Ankara.

TURKEY'S SHIFTING SIGNIFICANCE

THE STRENGTHENING of American influence in the southern Balkans began after Bulgaria's revolution of 1989, after which the United States intensified its interest in Bulgarian domestic politics. Following communism's collapse in Albania, the United States again invested an inordinate amount of diplomatic capital in a relatively obscure Balkan state, a move that slowly eroded the political influence of Italy and Greece and the military influence of France and Britain. As Albania's ties with the United States have become closer, so has its relationship with Ankara.

The American fascination with picaresque and slightly wacky Balkan bit players was due partly to the shift in Turkey's geostrategic significance after 1989 and partly to a misinterpretation of the Yugoslavian conflict that has been adjusted somewhat since Richard Holbrooke's appointment as assistant U.S. secretary of state. Until 1989, Turkey was important mainly for its role as the most southeasterly bulwark against Soviet access to the Mediterranean Sea and as the only large secular democracy with an overwhelmingly Muslim population. Since the collapse of the Soviet Union, Turkey's role has changed. It has competed energetically but largely in vain with Russia for influence in the Caucasus and former Soviet Central Asia. Despite this failure, its voice is not disregarded, especially in complex matters like the route of the proposed pipeline that would transport oil from Azerbaijan to the West.

The U.S. viewed the Balkans as a problem of blood lust, rather than of territorial expansion.

The United States considers Turkey vital to blocking Iranian and Iraqi influence in the region. It served as a base for U.N. operations inside northern Iraq while fighting a vicious war against its own Kurdish population in the southeast of the country. The value of Turkish support for the Middle East peace process would immediately become evident if it were withdrawn. In the Balkans, Turkey's troops are participating in authorized peacekeeping, and Turkey's diplomats, together with the Americans, are attempting to soothe the bitter relationship between Bosnia and Croatia. Turkey has also committed to supplying Albania with weaponry and other military supplies should Albania find itself at war with Serbia over Kosovo.

Dramatic changes in Europe have had a profound impact on domestic Turkish politics. Failed economic stabilization policies, particularly of the current Çiller government, have fueled the electoral successes of the Islamic Welfare Party. But disaffection with traditional secular politics has been strengthened by a widespread perception that the wars in Bosnia and Chechnya are Christian crusades against helpless Muslim populations (and that the West is standing by and letting them happen). Although less radical than other political movements, such as Iran's clerics, Algeria's Islamic Salvation Front, and Egypt's Muslim Brotherhood, Turkey's Welfare Party could jeopardize American interests in the region were it to become the leading force in Turkish politics.

The United States' increased interest in the southern Balkans was prompted primarily by its concern about Turkey. However, during the Bush administration and the first half of President Clinton's term, there were indications that the policy was also informed by a desire to isolate Serbia. During that time U.S. policymakers appeared to believe that the spark that could light a wider Balkan war was not Macedonia but Kosovo. This was due in part to the misperception that irrational blood lust rather than calculated territorial expansion was the cause of the Balkan conflict. Warnings issued by both Bush and Clinton to the Serbian government not to stir up trouble in Kosovo were redundant. Serbian President Slobodan Milošević had no intention of opening up a southern front of military conflict on territory that the Serbs already controlled. The U.S. stress on Kosovo was due in part to the pronounced Albanophilia and Serbophobia within State Department ranks.

American attention first focused on the fragility of Macedonia and the ambiguous Albanian role there in early 1994, when Albania's state-controlled media began supporting radicals in the Albanian community of western Macedonia. These radicals wanted no participation by the ethnic Albanians' Democratic Prosperity Party in Macedonia's governing coalition. Understanding the incendiary potential of polarization, American officials warned against meddling, and Albanian President Sali Berisha did as he was told and snuggled back up to his benefactors. Since this incident, American policy has shifted away from the issue of Kosovo and toward four more likely flash points: Albanian-Greek relations, the Macedonian question, and the two Turkish-Greek disputes, over the Aegean and over Cyprus.

A DELICATE BALANCING ACT

AMERICAN DIPLOMATS are working hard to reverse the growing polarization of Greek and Turkish positions and to keep those tension from exacerbating the Aegean and Cyprus disputes. One senior

U.S. official in Washington explained that "in order to keep Turkey happy, we have become involved in a delicate balancing act in the southern Balkans. If you appear to favor Turkey too much, Greece becomes nervous and so you need to find a way to calm Athens."

The U.S. State Department has put the juggling act required in the region into the capable hands of three envoys. In negotiating with Greece and Macedonia, Matthew Nimetz has exhibited patience, skill, and an ability to gain both parties' trust, but has yet to overcome the diplomatic gulf between the two and achieve a lifting of the Greek blockade of Macedonia. Richard Shifter sought to broker a normalization of Greek-Albanian relations, and America's overall diplomacy has now borne real fruit. Fresh mediation between Greece and Turkey by U.S. special representative Richard Beattie on the divisive Cyprus issue is just getting under way. President Clinton has supported his envoys with letters to the region's political leaders and given special attention to the war-threatening controversy between Greece and Turkey over Greek territorial claims in the Aegean Sea. He has sent letters to the prime ministers of both countries and dispatched a U.S. battle cruiser to the scene.

Operating largely outside the auspices of NATO, the U.S. Defense Department has stationed two spy planes in northern Albania to monitor troop movements in Bosnia and Serbia. In addition, it has deployed 500 marines in Macedonia, who operate largely on orders from Washington, not from the U.N. peacekeeping mission of which they are theoretically a part. More recently, Clinton has lifted the arms embargo on Romania, Albania, and Bulgaria and promised increased military cooperation between Macedonia and the United States.

This activity may not yet amount to a coherent military strategy for the southern Balkans, but it cannot be entirely haphazard. In the minds of government officials of the southern Balkan region, it makes sense. From Belgrade to Ankara, they are convinced that the United States has a grand regional design. Although each government has a different interpretation, they all exaggerate the importance of even the most innocent American move, increasing expectations of and alarm over American policy.

A MATTER OF URGENCY

THE UNITED STATES is still unsure how to deal with the most likely cause of instability in the region—relations between ethnic Albanians and Macedonians inside Macedonia. There are now strong indications that Washington understands this to be a matter of some urgency. Since the elections in Macedonia last October, ethnic Albanians and Macedonians have clashed over the former's attempt to establish an Albanian-language university in Tetovo, the center of Albanian politics in Macedonia. In January, the leading moderate in the PDP, Abdurahman Aliti, warned in an interview that his party might walk out of both the governing coalition and the parliament in Skopje as a possible prelude to establishing an Albanian assembly in Tetovo. In early February, fears of a breakdown were confirmed when Haliti resigned as vice chairman of parliament over a dispute about the use of identification cards in Macedonia.

Unfortunately, the U.S. mission in Skopje is very weak and has contributed little to attempts at settling the university dispute. If the United States is unable to bring the two sides together and reduce the growing tension in Macedonia, much of its good diplomatic work in the area will have been wasted.

American policy in the region is not borne of altruism but of a clear understanding of Washington's interests. The southern Balkans region remains exceptionally unstable, and its myriad conflicts are probably more than one foreign service can cope with, especially while more pressing catastrophes are nearby. One reason the U.S. State Department has sought to dissuade Croatia from expelling U.N. peacekeepers there is that a massive escalation of fighting in Croatia and Bosnia, which most international agencies fear would result, would further threaten Macedonia's stability. Nonetheless, the United States has done more in the southern Balkans than anybody else and is to be congratulated for its perspicacity. This has been a quiet, if crucially unfinished, triumph for which the Clinton administration deserves due credit.

The Triage of Dayton

Warren Bass

NOT A TRIUMPH

On November 16, 1995, Lieutenant General Wesley Clark sat in Dayton, Ohio, in a PowerScene virtual reality imaging system, using a joystick to fly back and forth through simulated three-dimensional scenes of the hills of Bosnia east of Sarajevo. At around 11 p.m., Serbian President Slobodan Milošević joined him, as well as some other U.S. officials. Lubricated by Scotch, Milošević and the Americans zoomed back and forth on the computer simulation to try to carve out a path from the besieged Bosnian capital to Goražde, a U.N. "safe area" surrounded by Bosnian Serbs. In the wee hours of the morning, Clark used crayons to draw a corridor from Sarajevo to Goražde that was not hopelessly indefensible. Milošević shook hands with Clark, who is now the supreme allied commander in Europe, and Richard C. Holbrooke, the main American peace negotiator, and what is variously known as the Clark Corridor or the Scotch Road was born.

Somehow, the United States had shifted from a determination not to be dragged into the Balkans to using U.S. officials and computers to draw Bosnia's new frontiers. Winston Churchill used to brag about having drawn Jordan's borders on a map one afternoon; the American general could say much the same thing about Bosnia. But America's entry lacked swagger. Rather, U.S. policymakers came to sketch the Scotch Road with a profound sense of ambivalence. Documents relating to this diplomacy—including Holbrooke's memoir *To End a War* and the State Department's 1996 official study of the

---

Warren Bass is an Associate Editor at *Foreign Affairs* and a Wexner Fellow in history at Columbia University.

process leading to the Dayton Accords of November 1995—show that American officials were painfully aware of the shortcomings of U.S. Bosnia policy and the distance it had shifted from the goals that Bill Clinton had espoused in 1992. If the devil is in the new details, they both afford a richer understanding of the evolution of U.S. policy and reinforce the enormity of the shortfall of American statecraft in the Bosnian crucible.

To be sure, Dayton was a vast improvement over the muddle and bloodshed that preceded it. But it has been oversold. Dayton represented not the vindication of the liberal ideals with which Bill Clinton excoriated George Bush on the 1992 campaign trail—firm action to halt genocide, bringing war criminals to justice, tolerance, multiethnic nation-states, liberal nationalism, and the use of international and European institutions—but rather a version of the chilly realpolitik that kept the Bush administration out of Bosnia. The deal the administration helped cut edged ominously close to partition, writing an epitaph for Bosnia as a multiethnic state and ceding much of its territory to the Bosnian Serbs. Many of Dayton's better provisions, especially the prosecution of war criminals and the return of refugees, remain largely unimplemented. Worse, Dayton required dealing with and ultimately strengthening Milošević and Croatian President Franjo Tudjman, two ethnic nationalists whose ideology and ruthlessness are antithetical to liberal values.

Dayton's lessons are grimly appropriate when considering the current violence in Kosovo, where Milošević's demagoguery helped set off Yugoslavia's demise and which is the latest target of his ethnic cleansing. The bloodshed in Kosovo is a symptom of the approach that strengthened Milošević and Tudjman. By doing so, Dayton plunged Serbia deeper into ethnic chauvinism, whereby the "sacred Serb soil" of Kosovo matters vastly more to Belgrade than do the Albanians living on top of it. As such, today's crisis comes as scant surprise. While the theater has shifted, and while Kosovo is part of Serbia proper, the underlying questions are much the same. As in 1993, the Clinton administration finds itself faced with a fundamental choice. Will the United States push Milošević to respect autonomy, the rights of minorities, and the rule of law, or will it retreat, as it did for two years in Bosnia, by saying that getting involved is not worth American blood and treasure? If it does back down, the retreat

AP/WIDE WORLD PHOTOS

E Pluribus Pluribus: Bosnian President Alija Izetbegović and Serbian President Slobodan Milošević shake hands as Croatian President Franjo Tudman looks on, Dayton Ohio, November 1, 1995.

must include the realization that the Clinton administration's earlier policy of realpolitik eased the way to future episodes thereof.

Winning any accord in Bosnia was not easy. Dayton took considerable diplomatic skill and tenacity. Congress' isolationists proved unhelpful and irresponsible, and the administration ran huge political risks by deciding to intervene. But it ran those risks for a reluctant realism. It is hard not to wonder what might have been if it had run them on behalf of the liberal ideals that it promised. In the end, the very policies that the administration balked at in May 1993—using military force and firm leadership of the Europeans—were the ones that stopped the war in the autumn of 1995. According to Warren Zimmermann, the last U.S. ambassador to Yugoslavia, the cost of delay was more than 100,000 lives. The fuller our picture of Dayton becomes, the clearer it is that the Dayton process—its accomplishments notwithstanding—is less a how-to manual for peacemakers than a cautionary tale.

THE BUSH LEGACY

THE CLINTON administration inherited a mess. Its Republican predecessors were consummate realists. After meeting Milošević in Belgrade in June 1991 to warn him against "exploitation of ethnic resentments [and] failure to respect human rights in Kosovo"—complaints that could be lifted from today's headlines—Secretary of State James A. Baker III felt he "was talking to a wall with a crew cut." The Bush administration greeted Yugoslav intransigence with a shrug. Its basic—and correct—diplomatic calculus was that only military force would deter the ambitions of Milošević and Tudjman. Its basic—and incorrect—political calculus was that such an intervention could never be sold to the American people. That assessment was shaded by President Bush's determination not to try. National Security Adviser Brent Scowcroft said that the president would frequently ask him, "Tell me again what this is all about." He saw no U.S. interests engaged in Bosnia, and his European allies reinforced his skepticism. "Once in, where does it end?" asked British Prime Minister John Major. Instead, the Bush administration treated Bosnia as, in Baker's words, "a humanitarian nightmare in the heart of Europe," as if Bosnia's woes were the result of a famine or an earthquake rather than an act of aggression. The bottom line, as Baker put it, was that the costs in casualties "would have been staggering . . . the necessary support by the American people for the degree of force that would have been required in Bosnia could never have been built or maintained."

Clinton, on the other hand, promised a very different policy on the campaign trail. "I know that ethnic divisions are one of the strongest impulses in all of society all over the world," he said, "but we've got to take a stand against it." The Bush administration, he charged, was immoral "for turning its back on violations of basic human rights," and needed to show "real leadership." When the Clinton administration dithered, unlike the Bush administration, it did so in defiance of its promises.

The war could well have been ended in May 1993 had the president fulfilled his campaign pledge to lift the arms embargo on the Bosnians and launch air strikes on the Serbs. At that time, Clinton sent Secretary of State Warren Christopher to sound out the Europeans about lift and strike. But Christopher was instructed to consult, not to lead, and what he heard was across-the-board opposition, concern for European soldiers in the U.N. Protection Force (UNPROFOR), distaste for supposed American arrogance, and warnings that NATO might sunder. At a pivotal briefing in the Roosevelt Room the morning of his return, Christopher told Clinton that lift and strike was still viable, but that it would require, as he put it, a "raw power approach": telling the Europeans "that we have firmly decided to go ahead with our preferred option and that we expect them to support us." Of all the choices, Christopher explained, the least attractive—and most hypocritical—would be to continue the Bush policy of "doing nothing." But Clinton blanched.

BLUNDERING INTO BOLDNESS

WHY, THEN, after two years of fecklessness, did President Clinton act decisively, backing heretofore toothless diplomacy with force and American leadership? Alas, the answer to this puzzle lies in a startling decision—or, better, a nondecision—that no administration should repeat. By the time of the August 1995 decision to push for Holbrooke's shuttle, without being fully aware of it, Washington had already committed itself to a military presence in Bosnia. The decision was made in so aimless a manner that almost all senior officials were caught off guard when the implications of what they had done finally sank in.

The State Department's Bosnia study confirms that most senior foreign policy officials, most notably the president himself, were surprised to learn in June 1995 that U.S. troops might soon be on their way to Bosnia whether the administration liked it or not. The confusion stemmed from an earlier presidential decision that, should the situation on the ground become chaotic enough to prevent UNPROFOR—the hapless U.N. peacekeeping mission already in Bosnia—from functioning, NATO would intervene to help the blue helmets flee. The Clinton administration confirmed this commitment in late 1994, and NATO military planners duly began work on Op-plan 40104, which called for using 20,000 U.S. troops as part of a 60,000-person evacuation force. When NATO approved this mission in the spring of 1995 with the consent of American NATO Ambassador Robert E. Hunter and U.S. military planners in Brussels, the Clinton administration boxed itself in. While an intervention to limit U.N. failure would be dangerous and humiliating, the White House figured that reneging on its promise to NATO would destroy the remains of its credibility and devastate an already frayed alliance. With the U.N. peacekeeping force daily revealed to be impotent, the only way Washington could forestall the withdrawal mission to which it had committed itself was to push the parties to peace—a better option, but one that would still require sending American troops to Bosnia. What one Clinton adviser called "the single most difficult decision of [Clinton's] presidency—to send troops to Bosnia" had been made without anyone realizing it.

The decision to intervene in Bosnia was made without anyone realizing it.

As the war worsened, the specter of Op-plan 40104 loomed larger. The Serb massacres of thousands of Bosnian Muslims in July 1995 in the U.N.-designated "safe areas" of Srebrenica and Zepa—the worst war crimes in Europe since those of the Nazis—made UNPROFOR's ignominy complete. European countries participating in UNPROFOR began warning that they would soon pull their troops out, triggering what American policymakers referred to as the 40104 "doomsday machine"—intervention triggered by humiliation. Several senior officials, including U.N. Ambassador Madeleine K. Albright and National Security Adviser Anthony Lake, began arguing that since American troops were headed for Bosnia anyway, the administration should try to implement a success rather than ratify a failure. As one official memorably put it, the question on Bosnia was not whether to stay in or out; it was "choosing which waterfall we will go over." Driven mainly by Lake and the National Security Council staff, senior officials spent the rest of the summer scurrying to come up with a plan. In August, Holbrooke's mission began.

The Clinton administration's decision to reevaluate its Bosnia diplomacy came not from a realization of the failure of its earlier rudderlessness or a renewal of Wilsonian principle. Rather, it came from a decision few could even remember making. When apprised of the details of Op-plan 40104, everyone—from Holbrooke to Christopher to President Clinton himself—was shocked. The choice to commit U.S. troops to help withdraw UNPROFOR was not the fruit of any formal deliberative process in which the president approved the mission through such standard means as a decision memorandum. Rather, it was made by inertia. If there were lessons to be learned from the earlier decisions not to intervene, they were not learned by the Clinton administration. Instead, it became bold almost by accident.

CLEAN HANDS

THE ACCORD that emerged from the haphazard process triggered by Op-plan 40104, as Holbrooke himself concedes, is hardly perfect. To be sure, it stopped the fighting, at least for the time being, which should not be underappreciated. But many of the problems of implementing Dayton stem from the way the pact was negotiated.

Holbrooke made a basic decision to ignore the Bosnian Serbs and deal only with the Yugoslav president, Milošević. Past negotiators, including the European Union envoy Carl Bildt and former President Jimmy Carter, had negotiated directly with the gangsters in Pale, the self-styled Bosnian Serb capital, without success. By spring 1995, American negotiators began to coalesce around what the lead negotiator, the late Robert Frasure, called the Milošević strategy. Washington would bypass the Bosnian Serbs and pressure Milošević to deliver an agreement. Frasure had noted the way that Milošević and Radovan Karadžić and Ratko Mladić, the Bosnian Serb leaders, had capitalized on their own disagreements to scuttle earlier initiatives, like a 1994 Contact Group plan. Belgrade and Pale, he concluded, had to be forced together.

The key would be the type of linkage that was a hallmark of Henry Kissinger—tying relief from the economic sanctions that Milošević so hated to cooperation from his Bosnian Serb friends. Although Milošević stridently deployed what Zimmermann described as a "clean hands" gambit—denying any knowledge of or influence over Bosnian Serb misdeeds—the Americans decided to expose his pretensions and tie any agreement to Milošević. When first introduced to the Serbian president in August 1995, Holbrooke made it clear that the Bosnian Serbs would be cut out. "You must speak for Pale," he told Milošević. "We won't deal with them ever again."

Milošević delivered, forcing the Bosnian Serbs to surrender virtually all their negotiating rights. The Milošević strategy held throughout the Dayton process. U.S. negotiators met only twice with Karadžić and Mladić, both times in Belgrade with Milošević as the principal interlocutor. At Dayton itself, where almost 100 negotiators spent 21 days locked in an area no larger than 3 square blocks, the Bosnian Serb members of Milošević's delegation were completely ignored. For the Americans, they were invisible; for Milošević, they were to know only what he chose to tell them about what he had negotiated on their behalf. Indeed, only minutes before the signing ceremony, Milošević told the Bosnian Serbs that he had given up the Serb demand for Sarajevo. Expansion into Bosnia's capital was the sine qua non for the Bosnian Serbs, and Vice President Nikola Koljević apparently fainted at the sight of the Dayton map. They stormed out of Dayton in an impotent fury without signing anything, but within a week an unruffled Milošević had them on board.

The Muslims and Croats are partners on paper only.

But within the success of the Milošević strategy lies a fundamental problem: the Bosnian Serbs are still not reconciled to Dayton. There probably would not have been a deal without Milošević. The dilemma is that, for Pale, Dayton is an imposed settlement. It combines appeasement—the Bosnian Serb land grab was rewarded with the ratification of Republika Srpska, the Bosnian Serb fiefdom, declared shortly after Bosnia seceded from Yugoslavia in March 1992 and one of the two major constituent parts of post-Dayton Bosnia—with exclusion. As such, the Bosnian Serbs have, unsurprisingly, balked on almost every major implementation issue. Although a more cooperative and moderate leadership (by Bosnian Serb standards) has emerged in the form of President Biljana Plavšić and Prime Minister Milorad Dodik, most Bosnian Serbs have no interest in sharing power with Muslims and Croats. The extremism in Bosnian Serb political culture has not abated. Whenever Pale has cooperated over the past two years, it has mostly been due to external pressures, whether from Washington, the civilian implementation coordinator, or Belgrade.

Dayton's handling of the Bosnian Serbs was an awkward dance, poised between contempt for and ratification of Pale's thuggery. One clear remedy would be vigorous prosecution of war criminals, including above all Karadžić and Mladić, indicted in July 1995 for genocide and crimes against humanity by the U.N. war crimes tribunal, as a way of remolding Bosnian Serb politics on lines other than ethnic paranoia. But Washington has moved only slowly toward greater activism on war criminals.

THE SHOTGUN MARRIAGE

THE MILOŠEVIĆ strategy was one key to America's Balkan diplomacy. Another was the creation of the Muslim-Croat Federation of Bosnia and Herzegovina, established in March 1994 as the other main constituent part of Bosnia alongside Republika Srpska. Bosnia's Muslims and Croats fought fiercely in 1993, but Washington sought to turn their glorified cease-fire into real cooperation. No other configuration could balance the Bosnian Serbs. Rather than trying to broker a three-way settlement (or, by including the Bosnian Serbs, a four-way pact), the United States tried to deal with only two parties: the Federation and Milošević.

The Federation proved essential in the negotiations. Military cooperation yielded results when Serb forces in western Bosnia were routed during August and September 1995, helping set up the Dayton chessboard. But creating even a semblance of trust proved excruciating. The two parties are partners on paper only. By the time Holbrooke's shuttle diplomacy began in earnest, there was scant evidence that the Federation could ever become viable. Late Deputy Assistant Secretary of Defense Joseph Kruzel, in his last report to Washington in August 1995, described the Federation as a "marriage of convenience" and warned that its weakness might prove the initiative's "fundamental conceptual flaw." Using the Federation to balance the Serbs was "not possible, because the Croats won't fight the Serbs over the Muslims, [nor] will they let the Muslims acquire enough weapons to be in any sort of position to challenge Zagreb." Holbrooke's team knew full well that even an "equip and train" program to boost a joint Muslim-Croat armed force would not erase serious doubts about the Federation's long- or medium-term viability.

Like the decision to cut out the Bosnian Serbs, the forced entente of Muslims and Croats points to a troubling paradox: the tactics essential to winning an agreement fundamentally undermined the ability to implement it. Notwithstanding American initiatives to build trust, the Muslims and Croats will cooperate only as long as it suits both sides' interests. Otherwise, they eagerly exploit each other. Republika Srpska is usually cited as the most likely cause of Dayton's shattering. But the most disturbing incidents of interethnic violence since Dayton have occurred not between Muslims and Serbs but between Croats and Muslims—ostensibly the allies keeping Pale at bay. The sleeping giant that could bring down Dayton is not Republika Srpska but the U.S.-backed and, to some degree, U.S.-created Federation. American diplomacy kept Bosnia whole by stitching it together like Frankenstein's monster.

DECLARING VICTORY

THE CLINTON administration, especially after it had found its sea legs, could show considerable diplomatic skill. It used Bosnia, for instance, to help advance NATO expansion by bringing Russia into the Implementation Force (IFOR). Defense Secretary William Perry and Deputy Secretary of State Strobe Talbott deftly negotiated placing Russian troops under direct U.S. command, even while the top U.S. general was also the NATO commander. This gave the administration the spectacle of Russian soldiers under NATO orders to point to as evidence that NATO expansion need not be anti-Russian.

Such skill, however, only reinforces the disappointment over what could have been, had the administration stuck to its Wilsonian guns. In a sense, the Clinton administration most closely resembles not the Bush White House but an earlier administration of Republican realists, that of Richard M. Nixon. Nixon won office in 1968 claiming to have a secret plan to end the war in Vietnam. Clinton, too, promised an end to the fighting in Bosnia, condemning the Bush-Baker policy—in Baker's memorable phrase, Washington did not have a dog in the Yugoslav fight—as pusillanimous. But he then abandoned lift and strike, intimidated by the potential costs, and let the war drag on.

Despite its own repeated warnings about the limitations of force, the reluctance of Europe, and the lack of an American stake in the former Yugoslavia, the administration did eventually intervene, driven in significant measure by its confusion over Op-plan 40104. The two lost years testify to the administration's belated realization that power is like a muscle: use makes it stronger. Had it led in 1993, the Clinton administration would have had more leverage with its European allies, not less. And the dereliction of leadership did not keep America out of the Balkans. It decided not to push in 1993 and then wound up stumbling into intervention in 1995.

Moreover, the form that intervention took was a far cry from the rhetoric of candidate Clinton. Having blundered into boldness, Washington lacked the raw materials to stay true to its avowed ideals of multiethnic tolerance, liberal democracy, and reversing aggression. By 1995, the administration had cost itself much of its room for maneuver.

This point is not widely appreciated. Indeed, many bristle at the notion that Dayton is an act of realism rather than idealism. In good realist fashion, it sees Bosnia as an anarchic environment and seeks to balance the Serb would-be hegemons with the Muslim-Croat Federation. The key decision to use the threat of sanctions to force Belgrade to deliver the Bosnian Serbs is a classic Kissingerian linkage. Moreover, Dayton dispenses with moral handwringing over tainted interlocutors and instead treats all sides—invader and invaded, democrat and demagogue—equally with pragmatism and *raison d'état*.

The claims of liberalism were sidelined during the process. True, there have been elections, and there have been some attempts by the implementers of the accord to temper Serb broadcasters. But reliance on international institutions proved a disaster in Bosnia. The European Union, for one, proved a reliable voice of timidity. But the worst failure came from the United Nations. Not only did UNPROFOR prove utterly useless during the massacre at Srebrenica, but the presence of U.N. peacekeepers actually prolonged the war by delaying Western intervention. The blue helmets were even taken hostage by the Bosnian Serbs. They also proved symbolic hostages when European powers with troops in UNPROFOR used concerns for their safety to blunt demands for air strikes.

The other major international institution involved in the former Yugoslavia—the U.N. war crimes tribunal, now led by Chief Prosecutor Louise Arbour, a Canadian judge—gets a more mixed review. The tribunal could only be as strong as the major powers were willing to let it be, despite strong leadership from its first prosecutor, the South African judge Richard Goldstone. Throughout the Dayton process, the United States underfunded the floundering tribunal, and since Dayton it has only haltingly pushed for prosecutions. Despite NATO's massive presence on the ground and the ability it demonstrated in its 1995 bombing campaign to cow the Bosnian Serbs, Karadžić and Mladić remain at large. Only at the urging of U.S. Secretary of State Madeleine Albright and British Foreign Secretary Robin Cook has the tribunal been able to make major arrests.

Finally, the multiethnic democracy of Bosnia no longer exists. What is left are the tatters of a tolerant, cosmopolitan society. Ultimately, the West lacked the will to reverse Serb and Croat aggression, and the Bosnian Serb obsession with self-rule was ratified, rather than rebuffed, in the form of the creation of Republika Srpska. Even the nominal unity of Bosnia as a state is a fig leaf. It hides the shaky realist balancing act between Republika Srpska and the Federation. In picking its Balkan partners, the Clinton administration did what it had to do, treating Tudjman—a Holocaust denier, authoritarian, and bigot—as an ally. Holbrooke's personal revulsion kept him from shaking Karadžić's hand, but the demands of realpolitik led him to swallow his distaste for Yugoslavia's main destroyer, Milošević, whom he sometimes portrays as an engaging rogue. At Dayton, much of the heaviest pressure was brought to bear on the aggrieved party, the Bosnian Muslims.

Churchill warned that "the principle of self-determination . . . comes ill out of the mouths of those in totalitarian states who deny even the smallest element of toleration to every section and creed within their bounds." He could well have been speaking of Milošević and Tudjman. These men were not vanquished by Dayton but emboldened. Many of the agreement's imperfections relate directly to the failure to confront the scourge of ultranationalism. Letting the Bosnian Serb entity be called Republika Srpska, in whose name ethnic cleansing was perpetrated, is ghastly. Dayton's core logic rests on a military balance of power and adheres to an ethnic territorial division—51 percent for the Muslims and Croats, 49 percent for the Serbs—that codifies Serbian aggression. At Dayton, the United States was resigned to the 51-49 formula; at one point during the talks, the U.S. team unwittingly negotiated a 55-45 division but beat a hasty retreat once Milošević found out.

The liberal elements of Dayton—a binding central government for Bosnia, war crimes trials, refugees' returning home, and a reaffirmation of the values of civic nationalism—will remain meaningless absent any determination to enforce them. Indeed, the ambiguity of enforcement is another key flaw. Wary of "mission creep," American military leaders prevented diplomats from committing to anything that might mean risking U.S. casualties. The military refused to take on the responsibility to enforce Dayton's terms, accepting only the authority to do so—an odd view of accepting civilian commands. Having finally made its way to an agreement, the United States squandered its best opportunity to implement Dayton's liberal elements by not moving boldly in the immediate wake of IFOR's entry at the end of 1995. In an election year, Clinton had no stomach for pushing the Pentagon hard to punish violations of Dayton. Thus, initially, Dayton's future was left in the hands of the very people who did all they could to prevent U.S. intervention: military leaders like Admiral Leighton Smith, the commander of NATO forces in Bosnia, who interpreted IFOR's responsibilities as narrowly as imaginable. In his first major local media appearance, after IFOR's deployment in December 1995, Smith assured Pale Television that he did not "have the authority to arrest anybody." Karadžić has passed through NATO checkpoints. Perhaps the most egregious incident occurred in March 1996, when Bosnian Serb thugs forced fellow Serbs out of their homes in Sarajevo's suburbs and set their houses on fire to prevent them from choosing to live under Muslim control. Ignoring both the spirit and the authority of Dayton, Smith ordered IFOR fire trucks to remain in their stations.

> Radovan Karadžić has passed through NATO checkpoints.

To be sure, things have improved over the past year, with more arrests of war criminals and the elevation of General Clark—the American military official with perhaps the greatest personal stake in Dayton's success—to NATO commander. Even so, the enforcement record is disappointing. Repatriation of those refugees brave enough to return home would restore some of the old heterogeneity of Yugoslavia. War crimes trials, especially for those atop the command chain, are also essential. An administration willing to risk the costs of intervention in the name of realism could run those same risks for a more lasting liberalism. Muscular enforcement of the Wilsonian elements of Dayton would be a payback, however belated and partial, by the Clinton administration for its May 1993 dereliction of principle.

In his memoirs, Holbrooke can explain the ethnic cleansers of Bosnia only by recognizing "that there was true evil in the world." As someone who was not even in government in May 1993, Holbrooke comes closest to admitting the full consequences of Western appeasement and silence in the face of genocide. His colleagues mostly remain silent. While few can be absolved of responsibility, the Clinton administration deserves its due. The political risks it ran were serious. Once it blundered into Bosnia, its tactics were skilled. Christopher and Holbrooke were tenacious at Dayton. But the decision to stay out for so long, the belated and muffed decision to intervene, and the acceptance of ethnic cleansing must also be placed at the administration's doorstep. Its Wilsonian pretensions remain as insupportable as its depiction of Bosnia as a foreign policy success.

Review Essay

Imagining Kosovo

A Biased New Account Fans Western Confusion

Aleksa Djilas

Kosovo: A Short History. BY NOEL MALCOLM. New York: New York University Press, 1998, 492 pp. $28.95.

Noel Malcolm's previous books include a biography of a twentieth-century Romanian violinist and composer, a volume engagingly called *The Origins of English Nonsense,* a history of Bosnia, and a life of a sixteenth-century Venetian heretic who studied rainbows. Since he seems to select his literary targets at random, it is tempting to dismiss Malcolm as a popularizer or charlatan. But in *Kosovo: A Short History,* Malcolm emerges as a talented amateur historian, trying hard—the book has 1,154 endnotes and a bibliography in a dozen languages—to produce a serious book about Serbia's southern province, with its almost 90 percent Albanian majority. He is only partly successful.

Can there really be a history of Kosovo? Malcolm recognizes at the outset that there is "something rather artificial about writing the history of territory, as a unit." But he argues that Kosovo has a geographical identity and is an important cultural crossroads. Alas, his account is marred by his sympathies for the Albanians and his illusions about the Balkans.

Kosovo was a central part of medieval Serbia, and Serbian kings built magnificent monasteries and churches there, many of which still survive. Still, Kosovo never had recognized boundaries. In the mid-fifteenth century, after its conquest by the Ottoman Turks, it became an ill-defined region within their empire. In the late nineteenth century, the Ottomans established

ALEKSA DJILAS is the author of *The Contested Country: Yugoslav Unity and Communist Revolution, 1919–1953* and the forthcoming *Yugoslavia: Dictatorship and Disintegration.* From 1987 to 1994 he was a Fellow at the Russian Research Center at Harvard University.

the *vilayet* or province of Kosovo, but it encompassed a rather different territory than today's Kosovo. Although after the First Balkan War of 1912 it was again part of Serbia—called then and now by Serbs Kosovo-Metohija—it did not become an autonomous administrative unit. Nor did it achieve such status after World War I, when Montenegro and the South Slav provinces of the former Austria-Hungary joined Serbia to form Yugoslavia, which, until 1929, was officially called the Kingdom of the Serbs, Croats, and Slovenes.

Only after the defeat of the Nazis in World War II did Kosovo achieve autonomy. During the war, the communist-led Partisan Army fought against Germans and other occupiers of Yugoslavia, as well as against rival Yugoslav military formations. While the Partisans were multinational and advocated tolerance and federalism, their Yugoslav foes were extreme nationalists who often collaborated with the fascist enemy. Some leaders of the Serbian royalist Chetniks, for instance, planned to "cleanse" the Serbian lands of non-Serbs. Their designs were foiled in 1945, and Kosovo began receiving self-rule. At first it was a mere *oblast* (region), but in 1963 it became a *pokrajina* (province), like Vojvodina in Serbia's north. In the early 1970s, the old Partisan leader, Josip Broz Tito, and his ruling Communist Party virtually transformed Yugoslavia's federation of six republics (Slovenia, Croatia, Bosnia-Herzegovina, Serbia, Montenegro, and Macedonia) into a confederation. For the first time, Kosovo, together with Vojvodina, achieved a high degree of autonomy and became in some respects—such as separate representation in the federal state and party bodies—coequal to the republics. These changes were finally codified in the 1974 constitution, which some constitutional experts argue conferred on the republics a last-resort right of secession; no one, however, claims that it accorded such a right to provinces.

Except, implicitly, Malcolm. He sometimes calls ethnic Albanians from Kosovo "Kosovars," a misnomer often employed by Western journalists and diplomats. There is no difference between Albanians in Kosovo and those in Albania, Serbia proper, Montenegro, the Republic of Macedonia, or Greece. Kosovar identity is as much an artificial construct as Kosovo itself. It is bizarre to name as Kosovars those Albanian-speakers who live in Kosovo next to the Albanian border, while keeping the name Albanians for those who live in Serbia proper, sometimes more than 60 miles from Albania.

Today Kosovo's approximately 1.8 million Albanians are demanding independence from Serbia, often with weapons in hand. The appearance of an almost 500-page-long "short history" of Kosovo calling them Kosovars can only help their cause. Readers will believe that Kosovo is a well-established historical-political entity and forget that Albanians are a minority within Serbia and Yugoslavia and not a nation, which would have the right to self-determination. Since Malcolm does not hide his sympathies for the Albanians and their struggle for independence, this effect was probably deliberate.

YES, ANCIENT HATREDS

Malcolm entered the field of Yugoslav studies with his *Bosnia: A Short History*. Published in 1994 in the middle of Bosnia's brutal civil war, this well-written book was an instant success. Not only did it fill the gap in Western knowledge about the most central republic of the former Yugoslavia, it also eloquently championed restoring Bosnia's unity and reintegrating its Muslims, Serbs, and Croats, who had been separated by war and ethnic cleansing. Malcolm maintained that Bosnia had a continuous history for almost a thousand years and was a distinct geopolitical entity even while incorporated into the Ottoman Empire, Hapsburg Austria, and Yugoslavia. Unfortunately, many of his misconceptions about Bosnia persist in his Kosovo sequel.

To Malcolm, it was irrelevant that Bosnia's Serbs and Croats were primarily loyal to Serbia and Croatia, not Bosnia, since at least the mid-nineteenth century. He also underestimated how deeply embedded in each of the three groups' collective memory were several major interethnic conflicts in the last century or so in which tens of thousands of civilians were murdered. In 1875, for instance, a major uprising of Christians against Ottoman rule and the Muslim nobility caused a major European crisis that led to the convening of the Congress of Berlin in 1878. During World War II, 400,000 Bosnians out of a total population of 2.8 million lost their lives—every sixth Serb, eighth Croat, and twelfth Muslim. More than half died in fighting between the three groups. Malcolm, however, preferred to stress periods of interethnic peace and cooperation. He assailed what he considered the myth that the current bloodshed was the result of "ancient ethnic hatreds," a fiction that he claimed was preventing Western leaders from intervening. Instead, he blamed the bloodletting on bellicose politicians, especially those in Belgrade. But the leaders of the three groups, while undoubtedly evil and guilty, could never have won over large majorities of their peoples for their chauvinistic designs if the memories of past suffering at the hands of the others and a hidden thirst for revenge had not been there.

Almost three years have passed since November 1995, when the United States brokered the Bosnian peace accords at Dayton, Ohio, but Bosnia is still separated into Muslim, Serbian, and Croatian parts. Hardly any refugees are returning home, and the common Muslim-Serbian-Croatian government in Sarajevo meets only when the West pressures its members. There are now about 34,000 NATO-led troops, including some 7,000 Americans, policing Bosnia and protecting the Bosnians from themselves. That the NATO force's departure is far from sight is a powerful refutation of Malcolm's belief in impending reintegration and interethnic harmony.

MY OWN PRIVATE KOSOVO

In *Kosovo: A Short History*, Malcolm is more realistic. He does not underestimate the importance of differences between Serbs and Albanians in terms of ethnicity, language, and religion (all Serbs are Eastern Orthodox, while Albanians are predominantly Muslim, although some are Catholic or Eastern Orthodox). Kosovo, he concedes, was not "always a wonderland of mutual tolerance." At the same time, his starting point is the same as in *Bosnia: A Short History*—"ancient ethnic hatreds" are not the cause of the present conflict. He then searches obsessively for those rare historical occasions when Albanians and Serbs fought on the same side rather than against each other.

But why, then, does Malcolm support Albanian demands for independence? In

Bosnia, he advocates restoring a unitary state. To be consistent, he would have to demand the reintegration of autonomous Kosovo into Serbia and the resolution of the Albanian-Serbian conflict through Albanian participation in Serbia's political life—giving the same prescription for Kosovo that he gave for Bosnia.

Malcolm fails to grasp the consequences of his inconsistency. While he chastised Bosnia's Serbs and Croats for refusing to fight for their rights in Sarajevo's parliament, he shows great understanding for Kosovo's Albanians' systematic boycott of elections in Serbia and Yugoslavia. But Albanian abstentions greatly harmed the Albanian struggle for their rights and the development of democracy in Serbia and Yugoslavia. Serbia's nationalistic president, Slobodan Milošević, all but extinguished Kosovo's autonomy in 1988 and, as Malcolm movingly describes, put Kosovo under police rule and fired tens of thousands of Albanians from state enterprises, the educational system, the police, and the judiciary. Albanians responded by creating a parallel political, economic, and educational system and avoiding military conscription and payment of taxes (their motto could have been a paraphrase of the slogan of the American Revolution: no taxation without representation). All Albanian political groups agreed to accept nothing less than complete independence for Kosovo and under no circumstances to participate in the political life of Serbia and Yugoslavia. But if the Albanians had voted, they could have decisively influenced the presidential elections in Serbia and Yugoslavia, and their representatives would have made one of the strongest parties in both parliaments. There they could have successfully fought for their rights and the restoration of Kosovo's autonomy—and even, through alliances with Serbian opposition parties, helped oust Milošević's socialists.

BLAME THE TURKS

Malcolm claims that the present Albanian-Serbian conflict has its origins in the First Balkan War of 1912, when the Serbs defeated the Ottoman army and, as Serbs still say, "liberated Kosovo after five centuries under the Turkish yoke." According to Malcolm, however, Kosovo was "conquered"; last May, Secretary of State Madeleine K. Albright said the Serbs "occupied" it. Malcolm vividly describes atrocities committed against Albanian civilians by the Serbian army, its Montenegrin ally, and especially Serbian paramilitaries. Other participants in the war—Bulgarians, Greeks, and Turks—also committed horrifying crimes against either civilians or prisoners of war. Serbian atrocities, however, did not create the "systematic hostility and hatred" between the Albanians and Serbs, but only exacerbated them. The enmity is rooted in centuries of discrimination against the Serbian Orthodox Church and oppression of Serbian peasants by Muslim Albanian lords and their followers—a point Malcolm lightly dismisses. He may be right that the main motive of the Albanian lords was the thirst for power and financial gain, rather than ethnic or religious bigotry. But the oppression would not have been possible had there not been ethnic and racial awareness and had the Serbs not been considered a different and inferior ethnic group.

Religion was even more important. As Bernard Lewis, the historian of the Middle East, has pointed out, the traditional

Ottoman political and social ethos "had its roots in classical Islamic law and custom, [and] was based frankly on inequality, since it would be inappropriate and indeed absurd to accord equal treatment to those who accept God's final revelation and those who willfully reject it." In the Balkans and elsewhere in Europe, Islam was often less fanatical than any Christian confession, but it nevertheless obliged Muslims to discriminate against other monotheistic religions. In both Kosovo and Bosnia, which lay on the Ottomans' border with their great enemy, Catholic Europe, discrimination against Christians was particularly harsh.

Even if the causes of the Albanians' plight had been purely political and economic, the Serbs would still inevitably have perceived both Islam and Albanians as oppressors and enemies. Analyzing post-1945 operations in Kosovo by the Yugoslav communist secret police, Malcolm points out that only 13 percent of the officers were Albanian, which added "to the increasingly bitter sense of ethnic polarization in the province." Of course it did, because Albanians felt subjected to alien, colonial rule, as did the Kosovo Serbs during the centuries of Muslim Albanian rule.

MYTHS AND FACTS

Malcolm was for many years a columnist for London's *Daily Telegraph*, which accounts for his lively, even gripping, writing. Unearthing the roots of the passion with which he tries to demolish most of the Serbian historical claims to Kosovo is much more difficult. He attacks the "myths" of Serbian history with particular zeal, including some that are not myths at all but only somewhat simplified historical narratives enshrined as symbols in Serbian collective memory.

Such, for example, is the "myth" of cruel and backward Ottoman rule, a myth that all other Balkan nations except Bosnian Muslims and Muslim Albanians share with the Serbs. It is indeed wrong, as Malcolm convincingly argues, to reduce Ottoman rule to barbarism, Muslim fanaticism, slavery, torture, and the suppression of Christian faith and national identity. The Turkish authorities, in the first centuries of their rule, often imposed lighter taxes than previous Christian rulers, interfered little in the details of everyday life, and made compromises with Christian churches. Still, the Ottomans and those inhabitants of the Balkans who converted to Islam had either monopolistic or privileged positions in political, military, judicial, and economic affairs, while Christians, both Orthodox and Catholic, suffered virtual social and political death through their loss of power and social status. Malcolm writes that "in the last two centuries of Ottoman power there were many cases of arbitrary rule, violence, and oppression," but he fails to mention that this was also true of earlier centuries.

In particular, Malcolm attacks the popular Serbian interpretation of the 1389 defeat of the Serbs at the hands of the conquering Turks at the battle of Kosovo Polje, or the Field of Blackbirds. He is, of course, right to point out that the Serbian army was not purely Serbian (the Bosnians being their main ally), that the battle was not a complete defeat for the Serbs, that their state survived well into the fifteenth century, and that its decline had begun after Emperor Dusan died in 1355. Yet there is a germ of truth in the popular myth. The battle was extremely bloody, both the Turkish sultan and the Serbian prince perished,

and the loss contributed significantly to the final Serbian collapse.

Malcolm believes that nineteenth-century nationalist intellectuals gave the Kosovo legend its nationalist spin, making it the defining event of Serbian history. Admittedly, this was the century of European nationalist revivals, for Italians, Poles, Germans, Greeks, Serbs, and Albanians, among others. But the nineteenth century only revolutionized national identities already formed by language, culture, religion, and, above all, history. The Kosovo battle became an ineradicable part of Serbian history immediately after 1389. Literary treatments soon appeared. The Field of Blackbirds inspired the greatest cycle of Serbian epic poetry, which was full of hope for the final victory and deliverance. The Homeric grandeur of these poems so captivated Goethe's imagination that he learned Serbian to be able to read them.

When Malcolm exposes Serbian historical myths, he actually uses the arguments of Serbian historians, who had disentangled most myths from facts by the 1930s. On rare occasions Malcolm really is original, as when trying to debunk the Serbian "great migration" of 1690. When the Hapsburg troops fighting the Ottomans were forced to withdraw from Kosovo, thousands of Serbs who had been on the Hapsburg side followed them rather than endure Ottoman reprisals. They later settled along the Hapsburg border, while the Albanians moved from their mountains into depopulated Kosovo. Malcolm attacks the authenticity of all elements of this story with perverse eagerness. As Tim Judah, the author of *The Serbs: History, Myth and the Destruction of Yugoslavia,* puts it, in his views about the migration "Malcolm is rather like someone claiming that the Mayflower sailed from America to Britain or that Ellis Island had little to do with immigration to the United States."

Malcolm's biases can also be seen in the fact that, of the 31 archives and libraries he consulted, none are in Serbia. He failed to visit the relevant research centers in other Orthodox countries, like Greece and Bulgaria, restricting himself mostly to Catholic ones, especially in Italy and Austria. Among the international group of people thanked in the acknowledgments, there are half a dozen Albanians but not one Serb.

NO EXIT?

At the end of his book, Malcolm writes, "Serbia had already lost Kosovo—lost it, that is, in the most basic human and demographic terms." To help resolve the Kosovo problem, the Serbs should recognize "that the territory conquered in 1912 already had a majority non-Serb population." In both instances Malcolm is right, although the Serbs would be more likely to accept his messages if he did not dispense them with such glee. (Its puckishness aside, *Kosovo: A Short History* should be published in Belgrade, where it would provoke a fruitful controversy.)

The Serbs' minority status in Kosovo has only deepened. In 1912 the Serbs represented over 40 percent of the population of Kosovo; today they comprise less than 10 percent. How did that happen? Malcolm wrongly believes that abortion is a "normality" for Serbian women and that therefore the Serbs "had only themselves to blame" for being outnumbered by the Albanians in Kosovo. But Serbian sexual mores and population growth resemble those of European and other countries where many secondary school and university students are women (in Serbia, the figure is more than half). In this respect, the Albanians are Europe's oddball people. While Malcolm shows little sympathy for Albanian women, kept in subservience by a traditional, male-dominated Muslim society, he does admit that with almost seven children per woman in the villages in the 1980s, the Kosovo Albanians' birth rate is Europe's highest.

Moreover, many Serbs left Kosovo during World War II and in the 1970s and 1980s, when Kosovo enjoyed a great deal of autonomy, because Albanian extremists forced them to—by murdering, threatening, taking their jobs and land, killing their cattle, felling their orchards, and even occasionally attacking their women. Malcolm underplays these causes for Serbian flight, insisting instead that Kosovo was simply poor and that better land and jobs were to be found elsewhere.

Despite Malcolm's errors in emphasis, he is right about the poverty. Kosovo's social and economic problems are so vast that it has to be granted considerable autonomy simply because Serbia cannot afford to subsidize it. Rural overpopulation is the main cause of Kosovo's poverty, but its once rich lead and zinc mines are also being exhausted. About half of the Albanian work force is unemployed. The costs of keeping numerous units of the Serbian police and Yugoslav army in Kosovo to fight Albanian separatism are also huge—especially after this spring's appearance of the Kosovo Liberation Army (KLA), a blend of a terrorist organization, a guerrilla force, and a popular uprising waiting to happen, which fights for the unity of all Albanians in the Balkans and declares political pluralism a "luxury." Finally, international sanctions imposed on Serbia for its repressive policies inflict incalculable economic losses. Serbian nationalism, it seems, is not only intolerant and bellicose but also bad for business.

With Belgrade in disfavor, all Western governments demand significant autonomy for Kosovo (without precisely stating what that means) and simultaneously insist that Kosovo cannot become independent because this would violate the borders of Yugoslavia, a sovereign state protected by the U.N. Charter and other international documents. The other argument they frequently summon, perhaps implying that the first one should not be taken too seriously, is that Kosovo's independence would engender further, potentially catastrophic changes of borders in the Balkans and its environs. Secessionist Albanians in Macedonia, Greeks in Albania, Serbs and Croats in Bosnia, Hungarians in Romania, and Kurds in Turkey would be encouraged, while Bulgaria might be tempted to annex Macedonia, whose Slavic inhabitants it considers co-nationals. The West seems not to realize that an independent Kosovo would immediately unite with Albania and upset the precarious balance between Albania's mutually antagonistic Geg north and Tosk south, which could restart the 1997 civil war.

Since its meeting in London on June 12, the Contact Group (formed in 1994 to bring peace to Bosnia and consisting of representatives of the United States, Russia, Britain, France, Germany, and Italy) has repeatedly demanded—with Russia the lone dissenter—that the Yugoslav army and the special units of the Serbian police, which have on several occasions used "excessive force," unconditionally and immediately withdraw from Kosovo. NATO, as well as the United States on its own, have also threatened military intervention and bombing. These Western policies not only encouraged the KLA but created deep divisions in the nonviolent Albanian independence movement.

Egged on by confused, biased writers like Malcolm, Western pressure is so intense that Kosovo will soon become autonomous. The main problems, therefore, are preventing the Albanians from seceding once Kosovo's political institutions are under their control, protecting the Serbs from being expelled by the triumphant Albanian majority, and keeping Serbian churches, monasteries, and historical monuments from being destroyed. The solution, if there is still time for one, must include some autonomy inside Kosovo for majority-Serbian regions and the most sacred Serbian holy sites, which together comprise about a quarter of Kosovo; an end to Albanians' boycott of elections and their rejoining the political life of Serbia and Yugoslavia; permanent stationing of numerous Western civilian and military observers; and a slow, Western-monitored transfer of the police from Serbian to Albanian hands, with perhaps a third of positions always remaining Serbian as a safety guarantee. But before a constructive debate can begin, Albanians must halt their militancy, Serbs must abandon their intransigence, and the West must outgrow its confusions—not necessarily in that order.